CREST
TO
CREST

CREST TO CREST

IMPRESSIONS OF CANTERBURY
prose & poetry

edited by
KAREN ZELAS

photography by
HENRY ZELAS

WILY PUBLICATIONS

Assistance with the cost of printing came from
Creative Communities Christchurch

Christchurch City

creative COMMUNITIES nz

Published by
Wily Publications Ltd
302 Lake Terrace Road
Shirley
Christchurch 8061
New Zealand
Email: jjhaworth@xtra.co.nz
www.wily.co.nz

ISBN 978-0-9582923-5-1

Photography by Henry Zelas
Cover photograph by Henry Zelas
Cover and page design by Quentin Wilson
Page layout by Antoinette Wilson
Printed by Sunny Young Printing Ltd, Taiwan

Contents

Plains

High Country

'...the soft white evening mists rising in the valleys and the distant summits glowing in the radiance of the setting sun filled us with admiration and delight. The notes and songs of the native birds, all new, filled us with a sense of enchantment and ... we came to the conclusion that the country and its scenery in all aspects could rarely be excelled.'

– Samuel Charles Farr (1827–1918), quoted in *Portrait of an Early Settler* by Diana Menefy

Editor's Note

Canterbury: from the crest of the ocean wave to the crest of the mountainous backbone of the South Island. The place where we stand. The place where we live, work, love. Our place. The place that defines us; the place that, if we leave, draws us back again and again.

Crest to Crest is a *kite* of gemstones, tumbled and polished, like those foraged at Birdlings Flat, spread glistening for our indulgence.

These writings convey something of what Canterbury means to the authors who have offered their work. Some pieces address the land directly, while others address the people who have or might have lived here, or who now live here and call it home. The collection forms a picture, one with spaces for readers to place their own experience.

No attempt has been made to be all-inclusive, nor to seek out the best of past writings. The emphasis is on contemporary writing, both well established and new voices, old voices and young. Even so, much outstanding and evocative work has not found a place in the anthology, and I thank the writers whose work has been turned down as much as those whose poetry or prose has been included. The selection process has been a highly enjoyable and privileged task.

I thank collectively the publishers and copyright holders of these works for allowing them to be included in *Crest to Crest*. Unless otherwise stated, work is previously unpublished.

The pieces in this anthology speak for themselves. Any analysis or explication, any drawing of threads and themes, sensing of resonances, or philosophising I leave to the reader.

Karen Zelas

Coast

in a wave
of sun
light

– Janice Healey, 'Still Remains'

Charlotte Jane, 1850

Frankie McMillan

captain's table
and its down to the last pig and sheep just six days before berthing at
    port
a stormy sea, deafening roar of the water, we jettison the table
    manners
harpooning potatoes, grabbing salt and bread as they swim past
neighbour in your plate and plate in your neighbour
a bad hand and pandemonium worse than the pig
on deck with a bone in its throat

steerage table
we stand at the galley fire on deck; swamped by waves and out of
    luck. what we eat is
sea pie. what we crave is fresh meat, a drop of milk for the little ones;
    the sarahs
and henrys who use up the canvas shrouds so fast we run out of
    weight
now it's lumps of coal to send them deep

on deck
nine swine, the milking cow too sick to yield
a dozen head of fowl, a crate of mustelids
and the twenty six sheep, long faced
as the losers of a card game

Note: The *Charlotte Jane* was one of the first four ships to land at Lyttelton, to settle Canterbury.

First published in *Dressing for the Cannibals* (Sudden Valley Press, 2009).

Still Remains
Waikuku

Janice Healey

i.
the sunless
bulging bellied bay

under and over
the moth/mauve sea
over and under

black pupae figures board waves
momentarily walk on water
other mothers' suns

sea change

years on   wave borne
the bleached
beached bone

remains
d.n.a. testing
talk of closure

old wounds open
fresh pages
bleed with words

over and over
the wait
wait

in a wave
of sun

ii.
no sound of a bone singing
the seabed cloaks
her treasure closely

where is the catch
the clasp
the closure

a toss of memories
polished as skin worn stone
ebb & flow

the touch
of his brow
on the palm of her hand

still
remains

light

First published in *Takahe* 58, August 2006

New Brighton Beach

Amelia Anderson

paua sky
shell crabs
sea storm, surfers ready
serrated waves
solo footprints
waving to his mother
the pair on the edge of winter

Note: Amelia is 12 years old; her brother was leaving home.

Putting Down Roots

Bettina Evans

Fiction

This story is dedicated to the memory of the first pioneers, especially the many women and girls whose stories remain untold. It is inspired by the remains of the mud hut built by Gideon Henderson, piper and shepherd, who emigrated with his family from the Shetland Islands to what now is Diamond Harbour, in 1874. The house, a short distance from the path leading up to Mount Herbert, is now roofless and slowly returning to earth. Surrounding the ruins is a large thicket of old and gnarly elderberry bushes.

After Mairie had pulled the tin from its hidey-hole in the thick clay wall of the milking shed, she hitched up her skirts and ran: away from minding the baby and knitting and spinning, away from the silence encasing Ma and the kitchen. Her bare feet slid down the steep hill. The sun had fried the grass the colour of griddle scones and now was dripping hot honey onto her skin.

Mairie jumped into her secret hollow and lay on the warm ground. She looked across Lyttleton Harbour, calm as Ma's blue Sunday shawl. Today Pa would be able to row the cream across the sea without spilling it.

She remembered her tin and shook out her treasure-bundle. As she unwrapped the scrap of material and searched for the wrinkled berries, images of the mother tree floated through her mind: the bush behind their croft on the island was crippled by the sharp salt wind, the harvest rarely more than a few handfuls because even the summer sun lacked the warmth to ripen and sweeten the fruit.

'Elderberries, elderberries,' she whispered, rolling the berries around in her hand. She nestled them back into the rag-bundle and scratched ten holes into the sparse grass, one for every year of her life. Into each hollow she dropped a berry. 'Grow-grow, grow-grow,' she chanted as she sprinkled earth over them. All she had to do now was to wait for the bushes to grow. She would not tell anyone about the seeds. Ma would cry for 'hame' and Da would frown and leave the house. The boys would tease her and the baby was too little to understand.

She ran down to the little burn where the trees with the strange names grew – ake-ake: a name like a sneeze, po-hu-tu-ka-wa: a spell, karaka: the cry of a raven. 'Ri-mu, ra-ta, ka-hi-ka-te-a' was a skipping-rope song.

The water flowed fast and clear and Mairie dipped the tin into it. She would have liked to poke in a stick and watch the fish dart, but the trees hovering over the water scared her. She had watched them through her first autumn here, waited for the first leaf's flight heralding showers of leaves, moulded leaf castles and finally the smoke-scent of autumn bonfires. But the trees had clung to their leaves. Da had explained that that was the way of the foreign trees. She knew better: they were magic because they were stronger than the seasons.

As she hurried back to her hollow, the water from the holes in the tin dripped onto her bare legs. She watered the first seed. She was glad that her elder bushes would change with the seasons: in spring, their branches would carry wool-tuft flowers left behind by straying sheep. She gave a slop of water to the second seed. When autumn came Ma would turn the dark purple fruit into a hot sweet drink. She dribbled the rest of the water onto the other seeds. In winter the bushes would be spent and tired like their cows and chickens, ready to drop their leaves and rest.

'Mairie!' hollered her oldest brother, Angus, from the house. 'Stop your silly games and do your chores!'

Mairie gave the seed-nests one more pat. She hoped the elderberry bushes would make Ma smile again, when she saw how they filled with fruit after a long warm summer. Maybe then she would not miss Scotland so much. In the hole in the shed wall was another tin with enough seed for a rose-hip hedge. And in autumn she would collect the seeds of the strange trees by the little brook.

'Coming!' she shouted and skipped up the hill, swinging the tin in her hand.

Quail Island

Apirana Taylor

no-one should be lonely
in life or death
no stone marks his grave
no words say
here lies our beloved
his twenty-five years
barely life's first breath
R.I.P. brother

rest in peace

Note: Quail Island/Otamahua was used as a leper colony in the early years of the 20th Century.

Apirana Taylor: *Te Ata Kura* (Canterbury University Press, 2004)

Towards Port Levy
For John

Mark Pirie

High in those hills your name is forgotten.
But the legend lives on in the yachts
Ghosting to anchorage...
   – Denis Glover, 'Towards Banks Pensinsula'

1
The hills, browned with the end of
summer, the four of us travelling in

the car. Congenial company, poets
for once in harmony together. We talk

of literary pursuits, our own and others,
gossip on about the 'good and the bad',

what's happened and what might happen,
and (always) in the back of our minds

is the past, memories of those
before us: Mick Stimpson, Glover,

and others, closer, now passed away. We
mention our mothers (both) now dead,

and highlight the day, the 'beauty',
'remember it', I hear you say.

2
Further on, we drive down the hill to
Port Levy, a bird catches your eye.

I scour the countryside for detail:
a row of trees, sheep along the hills,

the children come out to play.
And then entering the harbour

in tranquillity, the sea a reflection of sky,
we walk to the graveside, our journey now

complete, and stay a while, recalling
the past, Glover's poem, and, of course,

the history, painted as ever on a single
gravestone. 'Remember it', you say. I do,

noting wryly Mick's grave, how it lies
there, 'forgotten', glinting at the sky.

Mark Pirie: *Poems for Poets: Dedications and Elegies* (Earl of Seacliff Art Workshop, 2004)

Caldera

James Norcliffe

the dangers of the path
along the cliff top at dusk:

a glittering sun in your eyes
a slippery track of dried grass
overhang of agave and bamboo spikes

and there in the sky
a single hot air balloon
striped like a beach-ball
rising like a bubble of love
high above the harbour

it's best to stop
to breathe for the moment
before you step into space

it is all too fragile

how quickly it drifts
above the black basalt dykes
how deeply the shadows
stain the clefts and gullies

but the headwaters are red
like lava you imagine
red like magma rising
and lava running down

and spurting forth into a sky
full of the sparks that are stars
the stars that were sparks
before time began

First published in *The Listener*, 2006

Spirits of the Harbour

Doc Drumheller

The hills are alive
with the sound of gunfire.

Ghosts of lost battalions
sing World War Two ballads
in abandoned bunkers.

Echoes of Asiatic bird flu
hover over the harbour.

In our backyard
shipwrecked skeletons lay fallow
like kayaks at the wood turners table.

Dreams of paddling
to Smugglers Cove
are exiled to a leper colony.

Whispers of Scott's
frost bitten fingers
linger around a campfire.

Beneath the morning fog
a volcano's dormant stomach gurgles
as Russian sailors taste
hokey pokey for the very first time.

First published in *Takahe* 64, August 2008

At Rapaki
For the Couch Family, 2007

Jennifer Barrer

I am sitting in my
black skirt
down by the foreshore
at Rapaki
holding a bunch of flowers
from my garden
picked for Moke Couch

who will be buried today.
Seagulls cling to the rocks
gently, gently.
Like the trail of a
silken gown the aqua sea
creeps up to touch the golden
sand enclave and rubs
the rocks with sea salt.
Above on the hill is Moke's burial place.
The tiny church is empty
Wild parsley trails through the
wrought iron fence
I guard it
holding fast to the memory
of standing there with Moke
and Wera praying for my
Ngai Tahu pupils
in 1969
Seagulls squawk geese gaggle
I pass the Hutana graves
where mallow flowers and periwinkle
adorn the grass.
I speak to Moke through
my flowers
The totara rata hebe beech and
kawakawa
are for you Moke and the tulip
snowdrop, hyacinth and daisy
for your loyal wife Harriet
She is weeping.
It is time to climb that lonely hill
for Moke Couch's burial
Water dimples and a cloud
covers the sun.

Lyttelton – Pilgrimage of Pain

Lorna Staveley Anker

Cleaving swiftly
our longship V8 coupe bore us
warm-enclosed in utter comradeship,
it was a winged thing.
Now those roads, hills are opaque murmurs
dutiful, clipped, barren solemnities.

Burdened and stale lies the low-ebbed harbour
dun-curtained the briny village street,
and every time the trip to the port is made
old ecstasies lie ruin-deep.

How could we know
that rapture cannot keep its swelling pulse?
There was no warning in the ocean's ebb and flow
nor hint of doom from blossom, hedge or field,
that you so soon an unseen part would be,
of earth and air and ocean, wind and tree.

On Godley Head

Barbara Strang

We park the car at the end of the road. The day has not decided to clear; it is perfectly windless; mist throws a milky veil over the scarred hills. Through it I glimpse the soft green of early summer. We take the right-hand path along the top and walk silently together, passing under some huge battered pines. The Pacific far below is a blank slate for our thoughts. As the strip of beaten earth between the thick grasses grows narrower we walk in single file. I sense we are drawing close to the edge of a vast drop; the path peters out. We come to an awkward halt – I take a stance on the bank above, while you stand below. We can see hundreds of birds, gulls, cormorants, terns, looping and diving in the sky ahead of us. I watch their manoeuvres, how a tern swerves to avoid a gull; their cries a cacophony, expressing all the emotion that we have not. Now you do say something. I see your lips moving, but my ears will not hear.

> sunlight over the sea –
> one tiny yacht
> sails through the heads

First published in *Kokako* 10, April 2009

Visiting Boulder Bay

John Ewen

A memoir

We are high above the sea. The track ahead is a slash, like a duelling scar across the steep-sloped cheek of the hillside. Above and below us, the yellowed grass is motionless and last month's glutinous mud now rises as fine dust around our ankles. Heat presses down, muffling all sound but the murmur of unseen waves below.

Taylors Mistake beach and its baches, the surfers, the sun umbrellas and children with buckets and spades are behind us. We have walked off the sand, up the path zigzagging past large boulders placed there by young men doing Saturday P.D. some months ago, stripped to the waist, revelling in their developed bodies and competing in strength.

Now further on, we and other walkers share the track with puffing terriers, glistening joggers and, until they reach their own track, cyclists in gaudy lycra. Everyone speaks as they pass, often with foreign accents. We open and close gates for each other and wait in turn at stiles. On each side of the track are grey-leaved succulents with pale red flowers, thriving amongst the dry straw and stone outcrops. Even higher now, the track skirts small bays where there are caves and holes in the volcanic rock, and further down the sea gnaws away, undercutting the land. There are no smooth surfaces; all is jagged, harsh, abraded and abrasive. A lone fisherman is perched on a rock just above the water; we wonder how he managed to get down there.

Safety fences and planked pathways take us past massive old mud slips. Around yet another spur and there, far below, is the first view of Boulder Bay, its handful of baches squeezed between the edge of the land and the high tide mark. In a gully above the tiny settlement, native trees and shrubs have been planted to anchor a large slip below the track, and their bright greens stand out against the dry, brittle hillside. This is a vulnerable area: today as we follow the path down to the bay, we have to work our way around huge holes caused by the collapse of the under-runners in the last storm.

At the foot, large gnarled pines shade us and we see the first of many signs that are the second distinctive feature of the bay. Large and hand-made, its 'Welcome to Boulder Bay' assures us that the bach dwellers do not see us as intruding. All the other signs scattered around the area are manufactured ones filched from elsewhere, incongruous here in their settings. Many of them restrict vehicle parking; this on a little shelf between slope and sea to which access can be only by the track or off the water. A street sign, 'Sandy Ave', stands before a boulder-littered beach with no sand in sight. There is a sign for 'Hugh Street' and one warning of a school ahead and, perhaps most out of place of all, a door that is labelled 'NZ Labour Party Kawerau Branch'.

We follow the narrow path past the baches. Their pockets of garden are tidy and each building well cared for. A couple of upturned dinghies lie above the only cleared access to the water. Otherwise, the foreshore is a continuous jumble of rounded grey boulders, the lower ones wetly black with a wide fringe of seaweed thrashing ceaselessly. There is no one about. In spite of the Welcome sign, there is a sensation of intruding, of entering a deserted village. We thread our way carefully as far as we can go, and select a flat-topped stone to sit with our food and water. Terns arrive, assess their prospects and leave.

After we have eaten, we loll about in the dazzling clear light and heat. There is barely a breeze. Our stillness contrasts with the waves' noisy and tireless surging over the lower boulders and the offshore rocks. We are becalmed, lulled into quietness, watching and listening.

Before each swell breaks, we see, backlit by the sun, shadowy shapes moving beneath the surface.

The sea is a rich deep green, the sparkle of the sun transforming it into a myriad of well-cut emeralds. Three ships anchored offshore swing slowly in unison as if they are yoked to a single tether. We look beyond them to the horizon knowing there is nothing out there for nearly half a world; nothing until the same sea lashes the rocks and seaweed of Chile.

Eventually, that time arrives when we should be stowing our rubbish, shrugging on backpacks and leaving. On the return walk we will be confronted by Scarborough Head and the city beyond, places where values are measured in dollars, not in isolation, nor quiet reflection. But for the moment, we feel cleansed and refreshed.

Supper at Taylors Mistake

Kerrin P. Sharpe

the awning is a
broken wing each step

a creel of lead
weighted hooks a

chinese fisherman
is reeling in seaweed

there is enough
to paint his house

max a large black male
short haired cat cannot

find the beach though he
hears the voices of

surf opening *phylum*
mollusca like

binoculars they bring
the word lost closer

Winter Incident

Jan Hutchison

A man and a woman
trudge towards the estuary.
Snow falls softly.
Reeds are bare in the wind.
Silence sinks below the fabric
of their overcoats.
Thoughts are in pocket linings.
They pass a caravan on the verge
then skirt an upturned bucket
with cast-off peelings.

Of the pukeko that suddenly
struts in front of them
flickering its tail up and down
fluttering white under-feathers
who will tell?

Afterwards either the man or the woman
will remember the pukeko
with wings folded to its body
remember the bird running to the marshes.
The other will remember half-moon
turnip peelings.

First published in *The Press*, Christchurch, June 2008

Fragments

Tom Weston

It is true they walk on the side
of the harbour, a road hacked into rock
and blotched with succulents, tree lucerne

flicking seed at fickle sun. And it's here,
too, they sing along the road, bellbirds
so precisely true the whole air splinters.

In this we find certainty, knowing the land
patterned with a light and careless ease.
Each time it is, we return to immediate detail,

letting facts find their place, trusting
the incidental truths of voice and tree
and bellbird, and song on the road snatched

from random branch, a plainchant,
a riddle, this seldom lode. Then wisdom comes,
walking the harbour in solemn form.

Tom Weston: *Small Humours of Daylight* (Steele Roberts, 2008)

Notes from a Godwit's Diary
A poem for voices

Year 3 Students, St. Andrew's College

I remember the smell
the sense of place
wide open sea

*

alone on the estuary
a purple and white cockle
the cliffs remember my shadow

*

I pull my beak into the mudflats
and feel the vibration of a million worms

*

a giant arrow of birds
moulting a coat of red feathers

*

the smell of crabs in mud
seaweedy and sandy
the cold air

*

the smell of shellfish on rocks

*

my beak caught in smelly seaweed
the water clutches me

*

the marine worms in Alaska
wait under sand for me

*

the wind rushes past my cheeks
my wings ache

*

will my favourite snow pile
be there from last time?

*

the feeling of sand reminds me of home

*

Alaska, my wings flap
a blade of grass

*

I hear the goodbye voices
they were soft voices
baby voices

*

I think of my young godwits

*

E noho ra

Aroha

Karin O'Donnell

Aroha? said my mother: What is love
but the sweep of the sea
in Pegasus Bay
as it shushes and swishes
and swirls on the sand
gathering up granules
in wide blue arms?

But aroha, said my father, is the snowy Southern Alps
pointed peaks reaching ever upward
while at their feet
forest and fern
and birds practise hide-n-seek.

No, no, said my brother, aroha is a harbour
its deep turquoise waters
safe for dolphins at play
a welcoming haven for ship-weary sailors …

Ah, aroha, said my sister (with misty green eyes)
lies in patchwork plains
unfurled in a perfection of shades
a colour-filled comforter on a marital bed.

Aroha? thought I:
Aroha is the warm nor'west breath
the blackbird's dawn babble
the wide, braided river, skimming flat pebbles
the familiar and new. Aroha
is simply the sum.

Dream Houses

Fiona Farrell

Dream houses have big views:
the mountains are framed.

Dream houses own the view:
lake, sky, birds flying to nest
on stone crags. A bundle of
sticks where the young huddle
naked, with stunted wings.

Dream houses subdivide
the view: the bare curve of sand,
the jumble of driftwood laid
down at random by the sea.

At the dream house, the owners
walk hand in hand and wear shorts.
They smile. They drink fine wine.
They live the good life.

They have two lives. The other life
is the bad life. In the bad life, they
never smile. They never walk hand
in hand. They do not dream.

Children do not live in the dream houses.
On a grey crag, a jumble of sticks, in a
house that is not a dream house, they
nest, ten to a room.

The lights of the dream houses stain the
dark, filling the empty spaces between
hillside and headland and the wild beach
where the dreamers walk, hand in hand,
straight through their own view.

Between Islands

Campbell Taylor

Fiction

From an island made to an island undone, my father ran halfway round the world for reasons he'd never say; to meet a wife he could only just love, have a son he couldn't quite like and never see his island again.

His island is a tiny diamond cut from the mainland by a river that dissolved the soft rock and created a white chalk icon to die for. My island has never inspired patriotic song or been home to a queen. Though a queen ruled it for a while, over a century ago, sat in her bach on Dad's isle, signing orders for my distant land. Osborne House? Yes: a subtle palace suitable for the Empress who defined an age and attitude. Victoria. See, he did tell me some things.

And my island was an island but is no more. The distant mountains wearied and embraced it, though it still looks like an island to me. If you go up the plains and look back you'll see, the island that once was.

*

We're travelling into it now, just him and me, round the outskirts of the island, past the farms and gobbling subdivisions blasting out to Tai Tap. Tai Tapu. Slowing down – a Tip Top at Tai Tap? Not without Mum's vote. He probably has perfectly good ice cream at home.

Accelerating, we start to climb up an arm of my island, past the poisoned lake, dead from toxic run-off. I let this fact slip but, actually, the swans don't look too sick.

'And don't you lot say that Ellesmere is crook? Looked like plenty of ducks when we went past.'

'That's not the point, Dad. The duck shooters have filled it with lead. Poisoned the eels. The local iwi knows.'

'Maoris?'

'Maori.'

The car drops a gear to take us in silence to the heart of my island, and some rare time together. It's been five years since I left, dragged north by work, pushed by a need to escape my swamp-city home and the fog that pervades a town founded in the murk of island greeting mainland.

'Used to be twice this height; these hills.'

'Oh yeah? So where'd it all go?'

'Under Christchurch, I guess. Wanna stop for a beer at the Hilltop?'

'You're driving.'

'One won't hurt.'

'I'd rather keep going.'

We slowly drop into the volcano that blasted my island above the waves, skirting round the harbour, hurtling towards our destination. This trip's my idea – it felt required – a chance to be together, to talk, to ask. He's old. You never know.

'What's the name of that river that sliced the Isle of Wight off from England?'

'The what?'

'You told me once that it used to be part of the mainland, but that a river ...'

'The Solent.'

'Right, right. So the river's still there?'

'Nah, it's seawater now. Between Cowes and the ports.'

'Well, I was thinking, there must've been a stage when the river became sea – when the island broke off. Would've been quite a dramatic change.'

'"Spose.'

'That's where you saw the invasion fleet sheltering before D-day?'

'Yeah. They were packed so tight you could've walked across to Portsmouth. One bomb and the whole lot would've gone up. Boom.'

'Must've been exciting. And scary.'

'"Spose.'

'Did you want to go with them – to Normandy?'

'Not likely. This is the closest I'll get to Froggy soil. Rue de Fifi. It's on the main street, up there.'

We crawl through Akaroa at a seaside pace. The winter wind ensures there are few tourists. Wrong season. Just couples looking uncomfortable and seagulls resting their wings.

'Up here at the corner, if my memory serves me ... shit.'

'What?'

'It's gone.'

'But I can see it, Dad.'

'Just park the car.'

We climb out into the cold and walk towards the old bakery we've come to see. I'd been here once before, as a kid, on a summer drive with him and Mum. The ice cream at Tai Tap, intended to placate boredom on a long journey, hadn't stayed down when we started winding up the hills, and each parent had blamed the other for the mess. I remember the silence and the smell but not the reason for the journey. Why drive all this way to a bakery?

'It looks like a bleedin' circus.'

Dad's bakery – where he met Mum sitting in the middle of my island, days after stepping off the boat – was now the Dolphin Cafe. A dolphin leapt across a rainbow in an attempt to update a colonial building.

'Well, I'm not going in there.'

'C'mon, we've come all this way.'

'I don't care.'

'Come on, Dad, just a cuppa – for Mum. My shout.'

Inside, the decorators have shown less restraint. There are rainbows on each wall and a dolphin on every table. Underneath each rainbow, a painting priced to hang around. Dad cracks a smile I can still see.

'Bloody goons. Who are they trying to impress?'

'Tourists, I guess. I think you can swim with the dolphins.'

'No. That is not correct.'

The voice precedes the owner as she steps through the bead curtain behind the counter. She's an attractive blonde, possibly still enjoying her thirties.

'This is marine reserve. You are not to harass the creatures. There are boat trips to view them from the appropriate distance. If you like to make a booking, the information centre…'

Dad turns to me and barely whispers. 'German.'

She can't help but hear him. I smile.

'Have you been here long?'

'Three months.'

'So you'll be looking forward to summer?'

'Yes.'

She folds her arms and I wonder if she sees me as my father's son. He steps forward and dumps a mound of shrapnel on the counter.

'Two teas.'

We go and sit down.

'Do you have to be so rude?'

'Me? What about her?'

'She was only ...'

I'm cut off when the owner walks up to our table and places a twenty-cent piece in front of Dad. He takes it. I smile. She stands expectantly.

'Two teas are four dollars eighty.'

'That's what I gave you.'

'You gave me four dollars sixty.'

Dad looks at me and slowly gives her the coin she has just returned.

'Here you go then.'

She pushes it back.

'That is Australian twenty-cent piece. This is not Australia.'

I don't want a scene. Not here. Not today. Not in front of this woman. I reach for my wallet – too late.

'Jesus Bloody Christ.'

'Dad. It's okay. I've got money. I was going to pay anyway.'

'No. You, you come over here – to my country – and tell me where I blinkin' well live ...'

'Dad.'

'No. I've been coming here for what, fifty years, and she marches in as if she owns the place.'

'But, Dad, she does.'

The woman indulges my smile.

'Not this place, I mean ... well, yes, this place ... it was right here where ... Christ. You can stick your tea up your bloody rainbow-bum.'

His frustration aired, he heads for the car and I lose any chance to ask my questions. I'm just as bad as her – her in the cafe.

And her. Mum. Just like her. Same nose, same face. Same ... distance? Yeah, we'd both buggered off, Mum and me. But so had you. In more ways than one. My unvoiced questions and rebuttals filled the silence all the way back to Christchurch.

*

There must have been a point when the island I grew up looking at and playing on was no more; when the alluvial plains, washed down from the constant mountains, stopped being across the water and started to make the soup that filled the gap. I guess you could find the exact moment if you tried. Maybe it's more exciting to think of the time when the separation was more pronounced, when a bold swimmer might have dared to take on the currents and undertow to emerge on the uncertain new land. But there were no people here back then, only fish in a narrowing sea.

First published in *Takahe* 49, August 2003

Birdlings Flat

Janine Sowerby

blown across oceans
migrants from the north
jostled for a foothold

built nests –
loose collections
of driftwood and timber

for generations
they have squatted
isolated and insubstantial

like red-necked stints
feathers ruffled
huddled

they stare at the horizon
from grey stones
worn thin

waiting
for the wind
to change

Note: The strip of baches along the shore at Birdlings Flat originated as a squatters' settlement and became the subject of a long-running land dispute.

Uncle Charlie

Harvey McQueen

Banks Peninsula, two large extinct volcanoes, juts out from the Canterbury coastline. Harvey McQueen grew up there in Little River, which in those days was the end of the railway line from Christchurch.

My extended family were keen on picnics. Many of these centred around the fishing expeditions of my mother's brother, Uncle Charlie, who was the local rabbiter. In easterly weather he put out a raft (now called a kon-tiki) at Birdling's Flat, at the south end of Lake Forsyth. To get bait he would set an eel trap in the river the night before, baited with a rotten egg or a lump of stinking, ancient mutton. Once the eels swam through the narrow entrance, they were trapped. In the morning he would lift the trap, kill them, cut them into pieces and bait the long lines.

The stony ninety-mile beach was treacherous: a hubbub of crashing waves and a confusion of spray and spume, as the long combers gathered power to batter the shingle, rattle the stones in the retreating surf and pound in again. One of Granny's brothers drowned there at the turn of the 20th Century. Once, during the war, a fishing boat from Timaru lost power in a southerly buster. Helpless, the men on the beach watched it drift closer and closer until it was dumped in the surf and every man drowned. With such treacherous seas and undertow, there was always tension as Charlie tried to get the raft out through the surf, slipping and sliding in the loose shingle.

Once it was out to its full length, we had a long wait on the treeless beach. Sun-hats were essential but there was the constant threat of a wind gust sending them bowling into the surf or beyond. Then came the excitement of hauling the raft in – coiling skates digging their tails into the shingle, dogfish galore, the occasional larger shark and usually several big fat slippery groper.

A shingle bank stood between the lake and the sea. Unless this was regularly cut, the lake would flood. The Council used huge scoops pulled by draught-horses, the great beasts straining in the sliding shingle to get a foot-hold while the perspiring men encouraged them to give that extra pull. Occasionally we were present when the channel started to open, the men quickly pulling horse and equipment to safety as the force of the water undercut the banks and widened the cut. Later they replaced the horses with caterpillar tractors – but the task remained dangerous. When the lake was let out, local Maori pitchforked up the stranded, wriggling eels into a dray hitched to a horse, and dried them on racks standing on the lake side of the beach.

Charlie and Uncle Tom, who'd married my mother's sister, had a boatshed and a dinghy at Jones Bay in Akaroa Harbour, a small rocky inlet between Barry's Bay and French Farm. When the tide was right the extended family would drive over to scramble down a steep clay track through manuka, buddleia and broom, to picnic on the beach and go floundering.

While the men rowed out it was my task to sit in the stern and play out the net with its sinkers and floats. Sometimes, while we waited, the men would row over to Onawe Peninsula to collect and smash a few mussels from the rocks as bait for us to fish with long lines in mid-stream – mostly for red cod, but every so often, to much excitement, a blue cod. Behind us loomed the peninsula – the plutonic plug in the volcano's core. Friesian cows grazed peacefully. It was hard to imagine that it was once the scene of a brutal massacre, as Te Rauparaha swept down from the North Island in 1832 to raid and capture the local pa, and over a thousand Ngai Tahu died.

Other times, we splashed in the sea in our togs while the adults sat round and gossiped over billy tea, bacon and egg pie and scones. Mid-afternoon, not too late – Tom had to get back over the hill to milk his herd – the net was pulled in, all hands to the task, with a few cod, the odd puffer fish, lots of crabs and usually a good feed of flounder for every household. That evening, Mum deftly handling two large frying pans on the wood stove, we would feast in relays on the succulent fresh fish.

Duck – It's Open Season

Karen Zelas

mallards greys scaups
paradise on the Avon
quark quark

her husband
quark quark
grey down on his chest
plucked pocked
carcass in hand

one pile heads and feet
quark quark
guts another
quark

she shudders
turns her back
quick quick

to heat the oven

Onawe Yesterday

Mary Fitzgerald

Mid-tide –
they skirt around
tuatara twist
of land along the shore
they curve
to the rhythm
of the rock
russet

On the spine
they are silent
each absorbed
in the weight of their footfall
on this tapu ground.
Like the skylark crouching
in the tussock ahead
they are fearful
of the instinct
to dart up
singing.

They shiver:
Old Spiny Back
guarding
the bones of Onawe
may rear up and thrust them
into this molten
volcano
blue

First published in *The Press*, Christchurch, December 2008

With Ample Rainfall

Harvey McQueen

A memoir

With ample rainfall, the Banks Peninsula hillside soils, a combination of wind-blown loess and weathered volcanic rock, were fertile from the ash of the burnt bush and rotting stumps, as well as sheep and cattle dung. The river flats were formed from flood silt. Small one-unit farms, very dependent upon the wife's labour both in the household and on the farm, were indeed the norm, a conscious political decision of the Liberal Government of the 1890s. As the children grew, their labour was put to use. Sheep and beef cattle grazed the hills, dairy cows the flats and lower heights; most farms a mixture of both. Mainly Romney Cross, the sheep provided fat lambs for the English market, with wool as a supplementary source of income. The beef cattle were either Hereford or Black Poll. The sheep and cattle farmers worked to nature's rhythms, tailing, dehorning (both bloody and noisy events), shearing, drafting; bursts of hectic activity interspersed with maintenance tasks.

Dairy folk faced a harder life, tied to the cow-bails for nine months of the year. A continual source of disagreement amongst cockies was whether Friesian or Jersey was the better breed for milking, while the few herds of Shorthorn had their own devotees. Most of the milk went to the co-operative cheese factory, though a few farmers separated and sent the cream churns through to Christchurch by train. At the factory they met and yarned each morning as they delivered milk by truck or cart and loaded whey for their pigs. Unless they were working at the vats (suppliers were rostered as part of the cheese co-op), they could take the day off to go over to Akaroa Harbour to put out the flounder net, join a working bee at the Church or school, replace fences or repair yards.

John, my father, farmed in Pigeon Bay. Shortly after World War II started and I turned five, he failed to arrive home on time for the hot midday meal. His back was broken in a fall from his horse. He lingered a few days before dying. Except for Mum's distress, I remember little of the blurred events that followed. Ever since then a woman's tears have reduced me to helplessness. The day of John's accident remains clear, but the day of his funeral is completely cauterised. The event must have been traumatic to an imaginative child, an unexpected ambush of grief and loss. It created a deep guardedness, a distrust of happiness – existence was not reliable. The present could not guarantee the future. John's death welded a strong sense of insecurity onto me – an obvious grounding for a life in education, an occupation that attempts to bring some order out of the chaos.

Mum and her two sons shifted back to live with Pop, her father, at Little River.

Uncle Tom's old whey-eaten truck laden with our furniture stalled near the top of the Pigeon Bay Road. Pop's Oldsmobile was right behind. A rope was attached, and Mum, Doug and I were left on the snow-covered bank, watched by curious heifers, as the rope took the strain. After towing the truck to the Summit Road, Pop came back to collect us.

If at school I learnt 'the three r's', back on the farm I learnt other facts of life. One was the simple fact of killing animals for meat. All three men in my life – John, Pop and my stepfather, Dick – killed the fortnightly mutton, as well as old sheep for dog tucker. They cracked the neck as they cut the beast's throat. Pop alerted me to the pig's shrill dying scream when it was stuck through the heart. Mum beheaded chook, duck and goose with one quick decisive axe blow – a clean execution. She refused to let the beheaded birds flap round headless as several neighbours did. Men skinned the sheep and scalded the pig, women plucked the poultry – constants of life.

All three men managed large vegetable gardens. I helped, probably hindered, as they planted and hoed. Each milked a house-cow. Although Pop had two separate cow-bails, he often used to carry the three-legged stool out into the paddock. As soon as the small Jersey heard his call, udder swinging, she'd run to him. He would feed her hay, and, sitting on the stool, milk her. Every now and then he would squirt some milk straight from the teat into my or a dog's mouth. The pet Canadian goose, wings clipped to prevent it flying, waddling up to survey the scene, once got the jet of milk aimed for me. Thereafter the stupid bird expected this as a milking ritual.

It was not all idyllic: I also recollect Pop coming in from milking with his sou-wester and oilskin dripping wet and warming his hands before Mum's stove. He'd leave two large billies for us and go on over the road to Uncle Charlie's wife, Thora. One billy was for drinking milk (unpasteurised), the other Mum set for skimming. We had rich thick farm cream on porridge and pudding, and plenty left over for home-made butter. Mum gave her butter ration coupons to Thora who made shortbread for the two households. The dogs drank the skim milk. Pop kept a pig once; it also drank the skimmed milk, but he hated killing it; he'd made such a pet of it. Childhood lore was that skim milk pork possessed more flavour than whey-fed.

Across the creek from our cottage was Pop's hay-paddock, full of red clover and drowsy bumblebees. Cutting created great excitement. Two big Clydesdales pulled around the cutter in ever decreasing circles. Anxiety dominated while the grass dried, Pop surveying the sky, fretting at the least sign of rain; until it was stooked he worried. It was great fun to slide down the stooks; no-one seemed to mind, though we were warned about the dangers of pitch-forks. Before long a tractor replaced the horses and a baler the stooks. One crop got damp, so Pop had to keep shifting the bales around to let them cool; shifting hay meant mouse-hunts. Haystacks and haybarns frequently caught fire – spontaneous combustion, people explained; it seemed one of life's wonders to me.

Breeding ewes got first attention if a cold snap set in; they carried next year's income. Fat lambs needed drafting, red raddle for those to go to the works, blue raddle for those needing more fattening. The frenzied call of lambs separated from their mothers is an omnipresent memory.

Dipping was great fun. Pop possessed a tip-dip, a rare thing then. The sheep loaded, Pop pulled a lever and the pen tilted, throwing the sheep into the foul-smelling dip with a splash. Occasionally, one would balance precariously on the narrow ledge and Pop would use his stick to push them in. He'd duck their heads under to make sure all the ticks were killed. The chute gate opened, the sodden animals clambered out, the dip streaming off their wool, to shake themselves dry in the draining pens. The rams hated the place. It took all the skill of Pop's dogs to get them up the ramp to the tilting pen. They would turn on the dogs, stamp their feet. 'Back up,' Pop would tell the dogs. Some-times the rams charged, the dogs jumping nimbly over the rails out of the way. 'Heel,' Pop would say, and Jill or King would go for the nose or ankle. The ram would hurry up the ramp, the dogs bouncing behind. Pop would pull the lever, the rams would splash into the dip, the dogs gazing over the edge, carnivorous mastery over lesser herbivores …

Each night before school Mum made sandwiches for our lunch, mutton, jam or marmite. As we got older Doug and I took over this chore. Mum spoke longingly of oranges and pineapples, but despite the war there was plenty of seasonal fresh food. We called our meals breakfast, dinner and tea, eaten off the oil-clothed drop-leaf table. If guests came, Mum put a cloth on. Breakfast in the winter was usually porridge, Creamota from the packets with Sergeant Dan on them, in the summer Kornies, 'everybody's breakfast', the radio ads told us. Most meals consisted of mutton, either hot or cold, mutton soup all winter, fried chops often, neck stew. Always with mashed potato, except for the Sunday roast. People ask if such a daily diet of mutton and spud wasn't monotonous. Certainly at the time it did not seem so; it was what people ate. Uncle Tom killed a pig for Christmas and Easter, so pork became for me the symbol of celebration. Mum made brawn, chopping the cooked pigs-head apart with a sharp tomahawk. Pop always ate the trotters. When the young roosters got three-quarter grown it was axe time for them, Mum and Granny saving the feathers to stuff cushions. Sausages were a treat, whenever Pop or Mum went through to town, as was corned beef.

In late spring Uncle Tom's black-currant bushes would be laden. For a couple of days we couldn't use the bath, Mum would be making jelly, the juice oozing through the muslin bags hung over large basins. Other neighbours had gooseberry bushes. In autumn we collected large field mushrooms in a bucket while during the summer we harvested watercress from the creek margins. At school they told us to 'dig for victory'. Pop and Mum did their share with their big vegetable patches. Each autumn Mum planted lupin and each spring she dug it in to add nitrogen to the soil. She planted three apple trees, Granny Smith, Red Delicious, Cox's Orange, lovely names …

When Mum married Dick we shifted to a farm at the top of Okuti Valley on the east side of Little River. The divide at the top looked down on French Farm in Akaroa Harbour. The house was large and old, weatherboard, with a veranda running along its western front and the inevitable red corrugated iron roof. Scattered behind it were a garage with a haybarn on top, store-sheds, an earth-floored stable and saddle room full of old harness and other paraphernalia not sold at the clearing sale, a fowl-house, a cowshed and a pig-sty. Beside it, the large orchard had pear and apple trees and a rampant raspberry patch. The first apple to ripen was an Irish Peach – a pile of tree-ripened fruit and a good book was boyhood bliss …

Mum says this was the best time. For that Dick must be given the credit – plus her own resilience and courage. She loved being out with him. The widowed woman blossomed again. I am pleased life treated her generously then – for Dick also died young.

Hugh Playing the Moonlight

Fiona Farrell

Hugh is playing the Moonlight
to the valley.

In swannie, shorts and
Thursday's socks he takes
the stage before kanuka and
jostling miro.

He begins to play.

The kahikatea in the balcony
adjusts the stars upon her
shoulders.

Tawai on the high terrace
bend to pay attention
and kowhai huddle close
where they can sway in
their yellow ear rings.

Lizard and spider
bird and fish
rock and lichen
creek and tussock
all hold their breath.

Hugh's fingers find the
notes like seeds sown
on the stave. He plants
them in the dark and
the music sets leaf.
It grows into a
supple vine,
looping
tree to tree.

There is nothing more
beautiful in nature
than a man
in a swannie
playing the Moonlight.

Note: Naturalist Hugh Wilson established the Hinewai Reserve on Banks Peninsula.

Girl with a Teapot

Coral Atkinson

Fiction

Late 1830s. Banks Peninsula.

The girl with the teapot has no escape. The air is thick with vileness. Stench hangs over the sea, hovers above the shore and gropes into the gullies. The bay is small and the hills behind steep and bush-covered. The girl walks close to the edge of the trees trying to distance herself from the stinking beach.

There has been a kill and a partly butchered whale lies on the sand. Men climb over the carcass digging at the flesh, gouging into the slippery blackness as if tending a garden. They are cutting blubber off the body in huge bloodied strips. Implements scrape and clang.

Jane grasps the teapot handle. The porcelain is smooth and reassuring under her fingers. What day of the week is it? Could it be Sunday? Not that it matters. Not here.

In Sydney they went to church on Sunday. Jane's father, Charlie Fuller – a gilder – cleaned the gold leaf off his fingers, scratching it out from under his nails with the tip of a kitchen knife. One day in seven his hands appeared pink and new. Jane's mother took off her felt house shoes and put on her kid boots, worn and twisted maybe, but kid boots all the same, and they went down the road, all eleven of them, or nine since Maggie got married and George became apprenticed to a blacksmith. Father made them learn the collect for the day on Sunday. If you recited it word perfect you got a piece of taffy from the jar in the shape of an owl on top of the dresser. Jane was good at the collects. At first she'd tried learning them each Sunday when she came to the bay, but the words got confused and the days dissolved into each other and now she didn't know if it were Sunday or not.

The sand below the dead whale is a dark wound of blood and oil. The men at work shout and swear. 'Bastard!' 'Bugger!' 'Give it bloody here!'

Jane's husband, Captain Quinn, is down there with his gang. He is gesticulating and shouting, though his words are lost in the wind. Seagulls and rats dart to retrieve fragments of the whale flesh, which litter the sand.

Jane pushes the teapot under the fold of her shawl. If Quinn sees what she's carrying he'll be angry. He'll swear. Call her a fool and rage about her 'running around with that pot as if you were some bloody old statue. The men will think you're daft.'

The men.

The men moisten cracked lips when Jane passes. The tips of their tongues slip out of their beards; their eyes ooze lust and malice. They hate the captain for having a wife and Jane for being there. She reminds them of soft skin, puckered kisses, girls left behind, pleasure beyond reach. The men mumble bawdy words under their breath and spit. The globs of saliva hang on the grass stalks for a moment before sliding to the ground.

Captain Quinn wore shiny boots. Jane watched the boots that first time he visited her parents' house in Sydney. Comely and blond as toetoe, Quinn had a silver-topped cane, which he beat against his legs to make a point. The boots clung to his calves and sculpted the deft shape of his ankles. Jane wanted to touch the boots, to feel the warmth of the flesh within. She yearned to put her lips to the leather and kiss the shod feet. Instead she sat on a stool behind her mother's chair making a beaded net for a purse.

'Opportunity,' Quinn said to Charlie Fuller. 'New Zealand's just crying out for the taking. Seals, whales, flax, timber, land, all yours.'

'Thought there were black fellows there, too,' said Fuller.

'Buy them off. An old pistol, a few pairs of slops and a couple of blankets keeps them happy. Got a bay, a whole bay, for that. Pretty place too,' said Quinn looking at Jane's elder sister Lizzy and smiling.

Jane wanted the captain to smile at her. He didn't. Not even when he got up to leave and she handed him his hat.

Lizzy refused when the captain asked to marry her. Said she didn't fancy him or being eaten by savages in New Zealand. 'Anyway,' she said, putting down the knife she was using to butter bread for the little ones, 'Tom Dawkins and I have agreement. We're as good as engaged.'

'Dawkins never asked my approval,' said her father.

'He will,' said Lizzy licking a glob of butter off her finger.

'You'd be better off with Quinn,' said Fuller. 'The man's got prospects. He's a presentable bloke and headed for the top.'

'I'll marry him if you won't,' said Jane remembering the captain's boots.

'You?' said Lizzy. 'He didn't ask for you. And you're only a child.'

'I am not,' said Jane. 'I'm fifteen, sixteen next birthday. Better to marry Captain Quinn and live in New Zealand than stick in service emptying chamber pots all day.'

'You're too young to get married, Jane,' said her mother.

But Jane knew she wasn't and the captain wasn't fussed; one sister or the other, so long as he didn't go back to New Zealand empty handed.

Once it was agreed there were the stockings to knit, caps, skirts, aprons, bodices and petticoats to be made and chests to pack.

Jane's mother took the blue and white teapot off the top shelf of the dresser and gave it a quick dusting with a rag.

'Have this,' she said. 'You've liked it ever since you were a little chickabiddy.'

The teapot had a blue design. Abundant foliage coiled and eddied across a white ground and a tree arched over two women. One was a European wearing a straw bonnet trimmed with ribbons; the other had an odd shaped face like a frosted leaf and slanted button-hole eyes. When Jane was a child she would stare up at the picture of the two girls; 'Janey and the strange one,' she called them.

Sydney was stiff with heat the day Jane got married. Inside the church was dark as gravy. That night in the second-floor bedroom of The Star and Garter Jane thought she'd die with pleasure. Captain Quinn bit her neck, crushed her breasts in his palms and rolled her hips between his calloused fingers. He called her Rosebud and Sunshine. He kissed her body and said she was his little brown hen. Jane suggested he take off his nightshirt and put on his boots.

'You're a sly one,' he said laughing, 'all wide-eyed innocence but saucy as be damned,' but he did as she asked.

After it was over Quinn stroked her face with his hand as if she were convalescing from an illness and sang a song about sisters:

'Jane was a Woodman's daughter,
The fairest of the three,

Love in his arms had caught her,
As fast as fast could be ...'

'Tell me about your house in New Zealand,' said Jane.

'What's to tell?' Quinn nuzzled her armpit. 'It's got a door and a window and a roof.'

'Only one window?' said Jane.

'One's enough,' said Quinn.

The day they got to the house the waves slapped the sand.

'Quinn's Bay,' said the Captain waving his hand, as the newly wed couple were rowed ashore.

The smell of oil and kill was everywhere. It flooded about in a nauseating tide. Jane, overwhelmed by seasickness and stench, vomited into the wind.

'The smell,' said Jane.

'What?' said Quinn.

The men on the oars smirked.

A cluster of rough buildings stood close to the water. They stared through the mist like wounds under a bandage. Behind the shacks Jane saw 'the house' – the door, the roof, the window. A hut squatting at the back of the beach, it was casually cobbled together as if built by moonlight. A dark-looking pig scratched about near the door.

'Home,' said Quinn picking Jane up and jumping out of the boat with her in his arms. Quinn's face was close. Jane could smell his sweat and see the individual hairs of brassy stubble on his chin. She thought of the night time.

Quinn carried her up the beach and into the house. The door and window admitted a slice of light. Jane saw a make-shift bed of timber and scrim. There was movement in the shadowed corner.

'Bloody beat it,' Quinn shouted putting Jane down and gesturing at the darkness. 'Haere ra! Kai tere!'

A figure clutching a scarlet blanket ran through the room. Jane saw bare brown feet and long black hair. Was it a man or a woman?

'Who's that?' asked Jane.

'Raspberry,' said Quinn.

'A servant?' said Jane.

Quinn shook his head and laughed as he fumbled with the fire.

Mornings came and went. Some days whales were sighted from the lookout on the cliff and the boats were launched. Jane was alone in the bay except for Boyd, the cook, Haddock, the cooper, and the boy, Joey Higgins, who she'd seen hunkered and crying behind a barrel.

After a kill the gang returned shouting and smacking each other on the back. Quinn put a brandy flask to his lips and swallowed long and hard. He pinched Jane's bottom through her skirts when she went to greet him. The newly dead whale lay huge and dense on the beach like an eclipse.

On fine days Jane put her shawl over a barrel which they used as an outside table; when it rained they ate in the darkness of the hut.

Boyd brought the food up from the cookhouse in a billy. With luck there was fresh bread but later the flour ran out and black things crawled in the cabin biscuits.

'You're not eating,' said Quinn his mouth full of food.

'It's got weevils,' said Jane.

'Doesn't do any harm,' said Quinn.

'It's disgusting,' said Jane.

'Grub's grub,' said Quinn.

At night the wind hurled itself at the hut, while Jane and the captain wrestled together on the bed, which smelt of damp and tingled with fleas. It was exciting. It was terrible. It was like consorting with a lion.

In the daytime Quinn belched and swore as he rummaged in his wooden chest for articles of clothing. He called Jane ugly names and shouted at the men. He hit Barney Marlow round the head with a walking stick for dropping a cask of rum in the surf, and kicked Joey Higgins when the capstan ropes tangled.

Alone, Jane held the teapot in her hands. She stroked the smooth china and considered the two figures under the fantastic tree. She thought of the teapot high up on the dresser in the house, which swarmed with brothers and sisters. The children jostled and thronged in the kitchen; they overflowed into the yard; they fought under the scented vine and the fierce Australian sky. Each time Jane remembered her home in Sydney she found she'd mislaid something; the positioning of a dent on a tin plate, the shape of the boot scraper, the sound of her mother sharpening the carving knife.

Down on the beach the men slouched at their tasks. Jane, hungry for company, stopped at the cooper's workshop.

'Better get back up above, Missus. No place for you down here,' Haddock said picking at a wart on his palm.

But always Jane could feel herself being watched. Wherever she went unseen eyes were on her, sliding over her face and throat, touching her bust, stroking her belly, and moving down to her knees.

'Who is it? What do you want?' Jane called into the empty air.

Below the cliffs was a cave, which Jane had never visited. She saw the men go there. Singly or in twos and threes. They scrambled across the rocks looking furtively over their shoulders as they went.

'What happens in the cave?' Jane asked Quinn.

'Keep away from there, do you hear?' her husband said.

A whale had been sighted and the boats were out. Haddock was not in the coopering shop and there was no one on the beach. Jane took off her shoes and stockings and held her skirts bunched in her hands. The rocks were rough and hurt her feet but she went on. Water washed towards her and broke over the stones.

There were noises from the cave – human noises. Grunts and moans and then a single cry. Jane crouched down and peeped into the darkness. She saw a woman's arm, the pale gleam of a man's naked buttocks, and something scarlet. Jumping away, Jane scrambled back along the rocks. She ran up the beach. Did Quinn visit the cave along with the men?

Up near the trees, her shift, which she had washed and put hanging over a bush to dry, had a hand mark on it. Big and dirty. Jane picked up the garment and began to cry.

One afternoon Jane came into the hut. The air stirred. A petticoat had been partly pulled out of her trunk; it hung dejected like a bird with a broken neck. A figure in a blanket stood by the fire holding the teapot.

The creature turned. Beneath long hair, where the face should be, was a mound of stippled, puckered skin. The flesh melted over the contours of bone turning the definition of brows, nose and mouth into a red blur of humps and hollows. Fierce eyes peered from the monstrous features.

Jane screamed.

'What happened to her?' Jane asked later.

Quinn shrugged. 'Burnt. Boiling water they say. Some Yankee bloke got jealous and chucked it over her years back.'

At night the face threatened Jane in her dreams. By day the raupo by the swamp swayed uneasily. Jane sensed the hideous creature was always about, waiting, lurking, watching. Ready to rifle, filch, too, no doubt. Nothing in the house was safe. But Jane only cared about the teapot. She carried it with her, laying it in a nest of grass when she hung out the washing or putting it on top of the rain barrel by the door. So long as the teapot was safe, Jane was all right. She could talk, eat, move, and work. Without it she feared something huge and dreadful would happen. She didn't know what.

*

Quinn comes up from the beach.

'Fool! Cretin!' he roars seeing Jane hastily adjusting her shawl. 'What sort of a mad sheila have I married? Give that bloody thing here!'

Jane runs for the house but her husband is too quick. He catches her by the wrist, painfully twisting her arm and shaking the teapot out of her grasp. The china vessel falls. It hits a stone and smashes. The white fragments lie like bones on the sand.

Quinn scoops up the broken shards. Jane cries and begs for the pieces to keep and mend. 'Please, please,' she says.

'Stupid bitch, caterwauling about an old pot.' He shoves the bits of china in the pockets of his coat. 'Stay bloody here!' says Quinn as he turns.

Jane stands still. She is numb with misery. Quinn walks purposefully to the water. He climbs out onto the rocks and empties his pockets into the deep, frenzied tide. He comes back singing.

Jane lies on the bed and grasps her knees. She rocks back and forwards sobbing. Quinn shouts and swears. He shakes her by the shoulders and kicks at the bed. Then he goes out; staggering in hours later smelling of rum. Jane lies looking at the rough weatherboards of the wall in front of her and the thin threads of light where the planks fail to meet. Quinn slumps in the chair by the fire and sleeps.

It is almost dawn, though still dark, when Jane hears the door open. She doesn't turn or move. She guesses it is Raspberry and she doesn't care. Not now, not anymore. Let her paw or pilfer.

There is the soft patter of bare feet on the earth floor and the captain continues to snore. The intruder is coming over. Jane pretends to be asleep. The footsteps are very near. They stop. Jane can hear breathing and something drops on the bed. The footsteps retreat; the door closes. Jane reaches around. Her fingers touch rough fibre. It feels like a bundle of broken leaves, but it is small and heavy.

Jane carries the object through the darkness of the room. She opens the door to the pale glow of dawn. In her hands she holds a small, roughly made flax kete. She reaches into it and pulls out three shards of broken china – the remains of the teapot. There is part of the fantastic tree, half of the spout and most of the panel of the two women. 'Janey and the strange one,' she whispers cradling the precious shards in her palm.

Behind the house a flash of scarlet breaks the green monotony of the bush.

Van Gogh in Canterbury

Siobhan Harvey

The spirit is alive
in Starry Night reproductions
which hang, like crucifixes,
in varsity bed-sits,
petit bourgeoisie do-ups
and nouveau riche villas
across Canterbury.

In such replicas, he's reborn,
picks up his paintbrushes
and begins to set the Crusaders:
McCaw, Carter, Laulala,
upon the terra firma of his canvas
as if they're men at work, harvesting.

Then he finds his Arles in Akaroa,
where Port Louis-Philippe's spectre
besets him with visions,
small prophecies, of fresh work:
Landscape under a Summer Sky,
The Rue Jolie Bridge at Akaroa,
Three White Cottages in Rue Balguerie.

Soon, forgetting sunflowers,
he forms a fresh muse
from Duvauchelle's sol-radiance
of kaka beak and kowhai.

Finally, like Rangi and Papa,
he brings land and sky together
in a blue-black darkness
above the Onawe Peninsula
where stars are birthed so crisply
they stand in place of him
and speak of things long dead.

First published in *Landfall* 215 (Otago University Press, Winter 2008)

On Viewing a Painting of a South Island Cove

Mary Keaveny Costello

View the blueness of the hillside
Vied by blueness in the water
Mirroring the bush-clad hillside
Mirroring the fern and beach land;
Clearest double beauty-image
Clear as are the spears of sunlight
Slanting through the forest's branches,
Golden on the tussock grassland.

Such a brilliance greets the seeker
Paid in colour for the searching.
All about the inlet's stillness
Hovers low a haunting message:
Men who dared to court this new land
Left a vestige of their spirit;
Who could see and never love it?
Who could fight and die not for it?
Could they pass this winsome inlet,
Could they pass and not remember
How indelible the blueness,
And how clear the spear-like sunbeams?
When the Maori warred their foemen
When they stamped the fearsome haka,
How the reds and blues of Nature
Daubed their brown and fearless bodies.
Blue for moko, red from ochre:
And when on a flax hauhoa
Carried by his sated warriors
Rode the chief of all the victors,
Flanked by rows of dread head-bearers;
Red the pouring blood of wartime
Flowing as the blue bay waters
Over sand and mourning grassland,
Shaded by compassionate forest.
Peaceful now and peaceful always
Is a cove thus formed by Nature,
Man alone is the destroyer,
Man who plans to be possessor
Never pausing to consider
Man is merely fertilizer,
And the land is constant never
To the hand of each usurper.

From a manuscript entitled: *August in the Placid City*, 1970s, held by the New Zealand Room of the Christchurch City Library.

Runners

Jane Seaford

Fiction

The beam of the headlights tunnelled into the darkness and Phoebe saw a rabbit running in front of the car, its tail scutting white behind it. She braked, drove slowly, imagining the pounding of the big hind legs, the beating of the frightened heart.

'Whasat?' asked Merlin from the back, leaning forwards. 'It's a rabbit,' he answered himself. 'Get it, Phoebe. We'll have it for tea tomorrow.'

'No,' said Phoebe. Merlin sank down into his seat, the rabbit veered off the road and her mother, sitting next to her with Aquaria curled up on her knee, gave a gentle snore.

Half an hour later Phoebe drove onto the grass behind the bach. She turned off the engine and sat quite still in the blue-black darkness, listening to the swish and whoosh of the waves crawling up the beach and then pulling slowly back. Everyone was asleep; even her four brothers sprawled together in the back of the car. Phoebe sniffed, taking in the crayony smell of boy and the salt and fish scent of sea and sand. This was the first time they'd been here without Dad, the first time she'd driven the two hours from Christchurch, the first time she'd crammed her family into the old car; her full licence was only a week old. Time to wake them, to unlock the creaking door of the bach and hope that the memories inside didn't spill out and start Mum crying again.

It was the next day, and Phoebe felt as if she could run forever. She loved the feel of damp sand on her bare feet, the clear light of early morning tipping the crests of the waves, the endless stretch of yellow beach, the emptiness. The cool, sea-fresh air filled her lungs and she imagined it as a kind of pure fuel that would keep her going all day. Nonetheless she stopped, panting a little.

She raised her arms and spun round; she bent and took a deep breath. Then, feeling an uneasy happiness, she knelt down and stared across the ocean at the far horizon. All this space, and just her in it. Here she was not the eldest child, the daughter of the hippies, the one who ran the family after the father left.

After a while, she put back her head and opened her mouth wide, letting out a loud, deep wail that went on and on.

When it was finished, she lay on the sand in a starfish shape, exhausted. She hadn't meant to make that noise, hadn't known she wanted to. She thought she'd been feeling fine. She sat up and stared back at the bach, the tree behind it and the parked car. Inside were her family and soon they would be waking and wanting her, knowing what needed to be done to prepare breakfast but somehow unable to do it without her there.

As she came back into the bach, Merlin was telling the others what to do.

'Arthur, fill the kettle. Noah, look for the matches. They're in one of the drawers. Titus, stop playing with the cereal...'

None of them was taking any notice, except for little Aquaria. 'What shall I do, Merlin?'

'You can wash that dirty face,' said Phoebe as she closed the door. 'And Mum, why don't you get dressed? I'll sort this mess out.'

'Shall I...?' asked her mother, shaking her head slightly. She was sitting on the easy chair wearing one slipper and thin pyjamas with holes in and missing buttons. Her hair was tangled and she looked as if all night she'd been dreaming sad dreams.

'I'd have left you, too, if I'd been Dad,' Phoebe said under her breath. But she sighed gently and forced a smile, feeling her mother's sorrow pull at her own heart.

'I'm trying, Phoebe,' Merlin said in his hoarse fifteen-year-old voice. 'They don't do what I say.' He slumped onto the kitchen chair with the broken back and looked down at his bare feet, bending one big toe upwards as if it could, somehow, offer comfort. Phoebe put her hand on his shoulder. Of all of her brothers, he was the one suffering the most from Dad's absence.

'You lot, get your togs on and into the sea. I'll have breakfast ready for when you're back. Remember that Merlin is in charge so do what he tells you. And make sure you all look after Aquaria.' Life would be easier, Phoebe thought, if they had proper names: Pat, Anne, Mark, Nick; those would have done. And there'd be less teasing at school. Maybe even Dad's leaving would have caused less comment. And another thing, there were so many of them. Six, and there would have been a seventh. Phoebe thought of the poor stillborn baby that had come too early, just a few weeks after Dad had run away. Not that he'd been much use when he was there, getting stoned and drunk. Having a good time was what life was all about, he said. He despised money, he said, but was happy to take it when it came his way. Property was theft, he said, but he encouraged Mum to sign the papers when Gran gave her this family bach after Granddad died.

Phoebe banged the wooden spoon on the table. In spite of it all, she missed him. He made them laugh, he played great games, told stories that never ended, let them know how wonderful he thought they all were. And most of all he'd made Mum happy.

Later, they played cricket on the beach.

'You can bat first,' Noah said, offering Mum the prized position. But she frowned and shook her head. Her eyes were glazed as if she wasn't sure where she was, nor why she was there.

'Mum will watch,' Phoebe said, spreading a rug firmly on the sand. She put a pebble on each corner to hold it down in case the wind came up.

'But,' said Noah, not understanding.

'That was kind of you,' Phoebe told him.

For a few days after it had happened Mum had said nothing about it. She pretended that Dad was still living with them, that he'd just gone out for a little while. But Phoebe had known he wasn't coming back. That first evening when Mum spoke, she had sounded as if glass was breaking in her throat, although the words she used were cheerful. Earlier, Phoebe had found the note, screwed up on the kitchen floor. After she read it, she'd gone outside and had stood leaning against the wall by the backdoor breathing in great sobbing gulps of air.

Slowly, as if she was a punctured ball gradually losing air, Mum had deflated. On the fourth day when Phoebe came home, her mother was in bed, there was no food in the house and Aquaria was missing. She was still at kindergarten waiting to be collected; Merlin answered the phone when the call came from Aquaria's teacher. He passed it to Phoebe and later she found him in the garden, crying and pretending not to. It was only then that Phoebe told him about Dad's note.

'I think I knew he'd run from us,' Merlin had said.

Now Mum sank onto the rug. She pulled her floppy sun hat more tightly onto her head and sat gazing out at the sea, smiling slightly.

The game started. Merlin was bowling. He took long loping strides, rubbing an old tennis ball on his shorts. Noah squinted, gripping the bat in tense hands; his mouth set in a serious line. He hit the ball and ran, as fast as if his life depended on it. Up to the second wicket and back again. He stopped, looked about and set off again. The ball was in the sea. Titus and Arthur were wading in to fetch it.

'It's a six,' Phoebe called out. 'You don't have to run any more, Noah.'

After a while Phoebe left them to prepare lunch. She opened the door of the bach, stood for a moment enjoying the cool and the quiet, the pleasure of being on her own.

Later, when they'd finished tea – a picnic under the tree by the bach – Aquaria, sitting between Phoebe's legs and leaning against her, asked: 'Why did Dad have to go away?'

'I don't know,' Phoebe said. The note she'd found had been short. All it said was that he was leaving; that it was time for him to move on; that he loved the children but he needed to escape. He hadn't said that he loved their mother. Phoebe had noticed that. Neither had he said he would be returning some day. But then, again, he hadn't said he wouldn't.

Phoebe wrapped her arms around Aquaria, wanting to hold her close and safe, just as Dad had done to her when she was little. He'd held her tightly, too, that last evening before he'd left. He'd squeezed her to him and told her that she'd be fine and that he trusted her.

'You're not like your mother, Phoebe,' Dad had said. He'd sought her out that evening, asking her to come and sit with him on the bench at the end of the garden.

'No,' she said. She knew she was not like either of her parents and did not want to be. At school, the teachers encouraged her. University, they said. You'll do well, they said. Be ambitious, they said.

Dad finished rolling his joint and lit it. He took a few deep drags and then he asked, 'D'you want…?' trying to pass the joint to her.

'No, Dad,' she protested.

He laughed. 'You'll help your mother with the little ones, won't you?'

'Yes.' Phoebe felt impatient. Sometimes he would ramble on, say silly things. It was embarrassing.

'You can cope, run the house, the family, manage everything?' he asked. He sounded as if he might be about to cry and Phoebe stood up. She didn't want to hear any more.

He looked up at her. 'Phoebe, tell me you can.'

'Yes. Of course,' she said, wanting to go.

He, too, stood up, opened his arms, put them around her. 'I love you most of all. And I trust you. You'll always be all right. You're that kind of girl,' he said. She felt as if she were suffocating in his embrace.

When he let her go, she said, 'Night, Dad,' and left him, almost running up the path to the house, not knowing that the next day he would leave them all.

'Maybe he'll come back,' Merlin said now, starting to gather the remains of their picnic tea.

'Do you think he might?' Mum asked, looking up at Merlin as if he somehow knew the truth about Dad.

'He won't.' Phoebe wanted to say. 'He won't,' she wanted to shout. They needed to accept that he was gone; Mum most of all. But Phoebe said nothing, not wanting to inflict more hurt. And maybe, just maybe, Dad would re-appear one day.

That evening, when the younger children were in bed, Phoebe went running again. It was now nearly a year since Dad had left, over a year since the last time they'd been at the bach. She ran by the sea. There was still no wind, the water turned silvery dark as the sun disappeared and she saw a figure running towards her. Perhaps it was, after all, her father coming home. She slowed down, calling, 'Hello, hello.' But the words were lost; they drifted, thin and unsubstantial, into the vast unfettered horizon.

Opening her mouth to call again Phoebe saw that there was no one there; it was just imagination. She shook the disappointment out of her head and carried on.

As night claimed the space around her, she thought, 'I will go on forever. I will not stop or turn back. I am running for my life.' She thought of the rabbit running the night before; she remembered a neighbour saying to Dad, his voice a sneer: 'You lot – breeding like rabbits.' Feeling the strength in her thighs, the healthy pounding of her heart, she ran and ran. She thought of her father running away and she began to cry. She knew then that when the dark became too dense she would turn back; she could not run from her family before they were ready for her to go.

Snap
Amberley Beach

Bernadette Hall

What if that wave were to stop
just there as it is, snapfrozen?

What if the blowsy wave flowers stopped,
a rip in the valance, each fine blue stitch
stilled holding its silver needle?

What if the sea did indeed stop
and all the *vegetable armies*, the grasses,
mad bunches on the stony dyke,

the lupins, their heavy perfume stopped,
the starfish, pale asterisk on the stony page,
the polyps stopped, their strange juices frozen?

What if the gulls and the terns all stopped
and the tiny black swallows
that zip up and down the mid-night lagoon?

What if the sun itself were to stop,
no longer rinsing blue from the loveliest ice chamber?

Then we would be the wonders here,
like the seals, little fallen angels in the dry valley.

The bones in our hands smoothed
like long white gloves, our fine pelt wind-dried,
gravel in our brain pans and our eyes.

First published in *Sport* 33, 2005. It was also given a film treatment by 3rd Party Productions, 2005 and was played on Artsville, TV One. It subsequently appeared in *The Ponies* (VUP, 2007).

At the Bay
Caroline Bay

Ruth Arnison

Rock pool seashore lessons,
listening to sounds
in shells

Talent quests, with most of
the talent hidden, but we
didn't care

Surf jumping. Mum in her
deckchair crocheting
shell stitch squares

Bathing beauties parading
at the Sound Shell.
Carnival Days

Sunburnt noses competing
with fireworks, lighting up
the night sky

Calamine lotion cooling
burnt skin. Embers of pain
forgotten by morning

when towels 'n' togs were
scrambled in readiness, for
another day at the Bay

Ti
Akaroa Heads

Helen Lowe

Cordyline on a windswept point   stark
each frond stabbing
sharp as a taiaha's blade
defying the elements
facing down the ocean – that vast expanse
conquered first by Kiwa
the far voyaging   salt encrusted
sculpted by endless distance
always looking   ever longing for land
lying over the next line of horizon –
the darker smudge of blue
lifting to green above the deep swell
the first sighting   eyes shaded
of that solitary tree piercing sky
above a coastal headland   marking
the moment of transition
the place between.

Notes:
Ti Kouka, the NZ 'cabbage tree'; scientific name *Cordyline Australis*
The Maori name for the Pacific ocean is Te Moananui a Kiwa, 'the great ocean of Kiwa', the legendary voyager

First published in *Blackmail Press* 21, April 2008

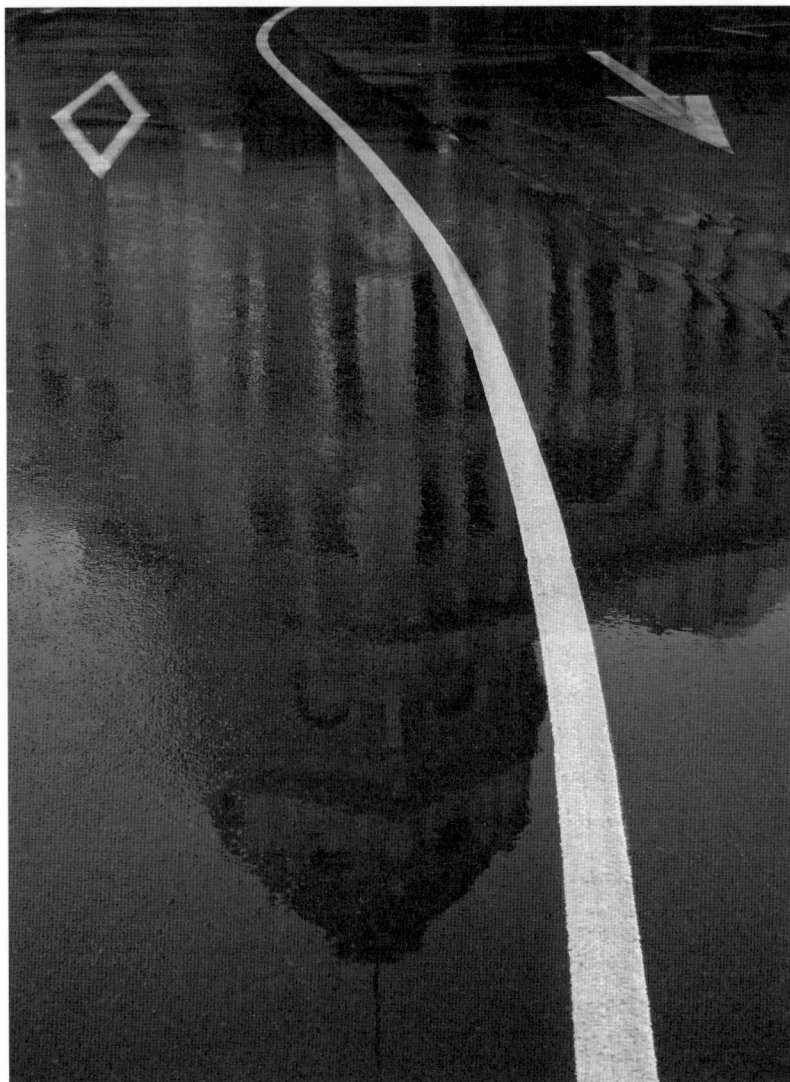

City

... a little piece
a cold jigsaw sound for a city

– Michael Hall, 'One Christchurch Evening'

Flying into Christchurch

Tom Weston

The day's frayed cuffs
scuff on the warm earth of evening,
insisting that cycles pass, expectations slipping
out over the mountains

burning their imprint into the cloth
of the sky, vermilion,
smoke wisping
from singed fibres as light surrenders

and the week ends. Across the plains,
flat angles rather than paddocks,
gaps where there are sawmills, shingle
pits, the whole commerce of the land

reduced to one condition. The rug
of the sea is rucked up and covered in dog hair,
unravelling at the edges where the surf
breaks onto wicker beaches. Colours shake off

so much geometry, with the rivers
carrying the burden of dying light
and the braided river beds becoming horses
or violent lovers, shiny as tin foil.

Who is to say there will be landing
when wheels scorch the asphalt, for it will
be dark, with pinpricks of light
and the terminal like all of Christmas?

Tom Weston: *The Ambiguous Companion* (Hazard Press, 1996)

Canterbury Settlers

Stephanie Lester

They pull back
Branches
Of unknown trees
Darkened beaches
And mysterious birds
Twittering among the trees
It is very still
Except for a slight breeze
They find somewhere
To sleep
For the night
They find some feathers
To sleep on
In the morning they will set to work on the new town
Their dreams

Note: Stephanie is 8 years old.

Portrait of an Early Settler

Diana Menefy

Samuel Charles Farr (1827–1918) came to New Zealand because he had fallen in love with Mary Ann Pavitt (1825–1912). She and her family were already booked to emigrate to New Zealand when they met. Farr joined the Pavitt family on the understanding that he and Mary Ann would be married as soon as possible after reaching New Zealand. They stayed in Canterbury instead of continuing to Auckland as originally planned because Farr had fallen in love with the land.

After a harrowing journey the *Monarch* finally reached New Zealand, berthing at Akaroa on 2 April 1850. Everyone was delighted to be off the ship. Over the next week or so, Samuel and five others climbed the hills behind Akaroa. He describes the country in a chapter published in *Canterbury Old and New*, the jubilee souvenir booklet:

We were charmed with all we saw: the vegetation in its primeval beauty; almighty giants of the forest overshadowing dainty ferns and delicate mosses: the musical waterfalls in the valleys leaping from rock to rock: rippling streamlets winding in sweet cadence amid the forest trees, entering shaded pools, or coursing through stable rocks and over rounded boulders on their journey to the sea.

Numberless were the changes as we sat and gazed, the soft white evening mists rising in the valleys and the distant summits glowing in the radiance of the setting sun filled us with admiration and delight. The notes and songs of the native birds, all new, filled us with a sense of enchantment and at the end of our ramblings we came to the conclusion that the country and its scenery in all aspects could rarely be excelled.

Samuel wanted to settle in Akaroa but knew it depended on a general vote. A meeting was held on the Monarch and forty-one of the fifty-two passengers decided to stay, influenced by news of the future development of the area. William Deans of Riccarton told them that the site for a city called Christchurch had been fixed and was being laid out by the surveyors. Ebenezer Hay from Pigeon Bay spoke about plans for settling the plains area beyond the hills Samuel had climbed, a huge area that was to be called Canterbury. He suggested there would be plenty to do when the first four immigrant ships arrived in December.

The decision made, Samuel rented a cottage on the hill between the English and French Akaroa settlements and set about making it comfortable for Mary Ann, who was still living with her family. He wrote:

I had no furniture and there was none to be bought in town, so I went on board, knowing they would help me with anything they could spare. An empty biscuit barrel, with a spare leaf from the saloon table, was soon arranged as my dining table. Four of the saloon chairs, which had been broken on the voyage, were lent, and I was to get them repaired by the time the vessel returned from Sydney ...

In the evening while the kettle boiled for tea, I made a pair of bow-tongs from a piece of hoop-iron taken off one of my cases, and finding an old musket ramrod I appropriated it for a poker.

I built an oven formed of beaten clay mixed with tussock grass. Then having made a bench, I constructed some stools, two easy elbow chairs, a wash-tray, and shelves of every description. For carpet I bought a piece of flax matting 9ft square from a Maori, so that home was improving every day.

They were married on 15 June 1850 – the first couple to be married in Canterbury.

Samuel continued his walks up the hills, often before breakfast to 'catch the early beauties of a quiet morning'. He referred to the 'wonderful works of nature and the still greater manifestations of an Almighty power as depicted in these magnificent hills ...' in defence of a panorama he'd painted from an outline sketched on 23 December 1856 by E. Norman. It was the 'birds-eye view from Mt. Bérard, or Coruonne [about 2500 feet above Akaroa], embracing what is now the whole province of Canterbury from the Kaikouras north, continuing [across] the Snowy Range to the south of Timaru.' The painting was exhibited in Lyttelton and Christchurch, and again later in the Canterbury Exhibition of 1870 ... In answering a critic, Samuel responded in a letter to *The Press*, 18 February 1870:

The design in painting the scene was to convey to future generations (although ever so feebly) that which was once the glory of the province. I refer to the wooded spurs and valleys as seen by us who landed just upon twenty years since. That beauty has departed, having been destroyed by the busy

71

hand of man, and still more so by the devastating power of raging fire …

From the paintings that still exist today it appears his favourite subjects were the views from the hills above Akaroa. He wrote:

The grand rugged mountains, with summits of rocky crags, reared themselves to altitudes around varying from 1500 to 2800 feet; ridges of wooded hills sloped to the edge of the placid sea beneath. Over the bay the water without a ripple, mirrored the forest-covered mountains with their soft purple tints. A scene so exquisite and fascinating could never pall …

However Samuel was indirectly responsible for the speed of destruction of much of this bush, as he designed the saw-mills that were used to process the timber, the first one being for the Pavitt family who had settled at Robinson's Bay. Samuel wrote:

Although I had never seen a mill, I had read about them and offered to make a model of one to scale, assuming that if the miniature form would act, it would be quite safe to erect a large one …

The full-sized mill was working by 1854, and when the Canterbury Association lawyer, Henry Sewell, looked over it in February 1855 he was much impressed. The Pavitts were earning £100 a month, excellent money for those times. But in 1856 both the mill and the house close to it were destroyed when '… a terrible heavy fire came down through the bush, devouring everything, and being furiously driven by the wind; it was only with great risk and difficulty that the saws and other movable tools were rescued.'

The mill was rebuilt and then the house. Samuel went on to help with sawmills set up in Barry's Bay, Duvauchelle Bay (in 1858 for William Henderson – later Cumberland Saw Mills) and at Head of the Bay.

In 1862 Samuel and Mary Ann shifted to Christchurch. He set up as a surveyor and architect, and was immediately successful in the local architectural competitions. In 1863 he produced the winning design for the Mechanics' Institute, which later became the public library, and his design for the Durham Street Methodist Church was placed second. As the winning design was from a Melbourne firm, Samuel was appointed supervising architect. Samuel became known as a nonconformist church designer; he designed St John's Presbyterian Church at Lyttelton, St Paul's Presbyterian Church in Christchurch and other churches at Papanui, Lyttelton, Kaiapoi and Leeston.

Samuel also won the competition for the Christchurch Town Hall in 1864, although there was little scope for his artistic bent. The brief required that 'all architectural pretensions were to be quite a secondary matter, rather than reduce the size of the room.' When the design was criticised after the building was finished Samuel wrote in response: 'Criticism has failed to prove anything contrary to its being fully what was desired: a good room for sound.'

Despite his success, when the Canterbury Association of Architects was established in early 1870, Samuel was denied membership on the grounds that he had not completed four years' training as an articled pupil under a qualified architect. This did not deter him and he went on to design many important public buildings in Christchurch as well as commercial buildings and private homes (the most noted of these being the mansion at Glenmark Station for G. H. Moore, and 'Hambleden' for George Gould). He also designed the first iron verandas in New Zealand, beginning with the one for Charles Kiver in Cashel Street.

Another aspect of Samuel's life was his involvement with the Canterbury Acclimatisation Society; he was appointed secretary in 1870 and stayed in this position for twenty-two years. He was instrumental in introducing the first bumble-bees to Christchurch to help solve problems in getting the red clover flowers fertilised, although it took twelve years of trying before the first live bees were imported.

During his time with the Society almost every lake and river in Canterbury was stocked with fish. In 1884 he sailed for England on behalf of the five societies (Canterbury, Otago, Hawkes Bay, Wellington and Waitaki) and brought back 120,000 salmon ova. He set up experiments to fertilise these ova, and was highly successful, about half of the ova producing fry for release.

Once he took 500 live salmon over Jollies Pass and liberated them in the Acheron and Clarence Rivers. On another occasion he spent five days travelling into the Southern Alps to release young fish in a small lake behind Mt. Torlesse about six miles from Craigieburn. In acknowledgement of his service to the Society the lake was named Loch Farr. We now know that these salmon did not return to their rivers after migration.

In 1910 Samuel and Mary Ann's family celebrated their sixtieth wedding anniversary in the cottage on Bealey Ave. Samuel was described in an article in *The Press* as being 'slightly stooped and his long beard as white as snow but he is an active old gentleman with a quick intelligence, perfectly sound memory and a very keen interest in things that are happening around him. "I suppose," he says "our married life has been one of the happiest married lives ever lived on this earth."'

Samuel and Mary Ann Farr were my great-great-grandparents, and in my youth I walked the same trails as Samuel and developed an equally deep passion for the hills and mountains he loved.

Canterbury Visit, Winter 1982

Keith Westwater

You clasp a shabby quilt
of dun and brown.

Memories from years before
at first stay locked away
like the snow water
in your mountains
marching north and south.

No storms call to your Port Hills
which are as bare as the trees
that trellis your sky.

But then, they always did.

Even as I enter the city
of my first true love
you get coy
clutch up a skirt of fog.

Once again
I have to fumble my way.

First published in *Yellow Moon* 20, Summer 2006

Landscape

Brigid Barrer

Alone we are born
  And die alone:
Yet see the red-gold cirrus
  Over snow-mountain shine.
Upon the upland road
  Ride easy stranger:
Surrender to the sky
  Your heart of anger.
  – James K. Baxter, 'High Country Weather'

My mother died suddenly this morning. On Sunday afternoon the aeroplane is descending over the Canterbury plains. My heart catches the patchwork quilt of green and brown fields, rectangles and squares, its ribbon roads and forest bands of trees. The Waimakariri is grey-dry with opal puddles, contrasting little kidneys of wet iridescence. And that is all the water I can see amongst the khaki clay sand banks and beds.

My mother died unexpectedly. I think it was around 5am, when I woke up at home; her heart stopped. She did not wait for my call at nine o'clock. When I sit down with the undertaker he tells me the shelter belts of macrocarpa, pine, poplar and willow are languishing. He is a tree man himself and has noticed my mother's two grown beech right outside the giant plate glass window across the road from the little park. My father died in December and now it is next October. Together they planted the trees to bring bush beech into this suburban garden. And now I am orphaned. She is still lying in bed waiting. I was the first to come and I have seen her alone. I have seen the bruises on her cold face.

On Friday she had a big fall, after going to the bank, then forgetting her purse and turning around and going back for it, then to the doctor, and for groceries. She lay on the kitchen floor for four hours until her visiting nurse found her at 6pm. Of course, she'd had a hyper-low, but the ambulance-men thought her vital signs good, so she had to have dinner and go to bed bruised. Her Saturday morning voice on the phone was quiet as she told me about her fall. I said I'd go down on Tuesday after my writing class. We talked until the neighbours were at the door, which was not long.

Beside the plains, the foothills are on show. My heart aches as the sun catches the snowy hills, the alps thickly white-carpeted. Three neighbours saw her well and happy on Saturday. One stayed while she had a shower. Her Saturday was freshly social with no hint of death. I thought she would have a good night's sleep and I would speak to her again in the morning.

I study the thin white hazy horizontal that divides the sea and the sky at the edge of the earth. Above it is the cobalt expanse and below the midnight shimmer of the sea. My heart remembers many Septembers I came to ski Mt Hutt. The bus would zigzag up through yellow tussock in mud, and, lurching round a corner, I would look down at the turquoise Rakaia and river stones through the walls of the gorge. Then, higher on the stony road into the snow and spring sun, the keas were already on the early cars. As I skied the day the whole of Canterbury's green eiderdown flowed out below me. At the top run we would take off our skis and climb to look over to the Southern Alps and on a fine day see Aoraki Mt Cook touch the sky.

My mother died as she wanted in her own bed, peacefully. She never went to respite care or a home. She had a holiday with me and bought art, saw the new gallery, and celebrated modernism just like the art on her walls. But I had planned summer with her in my head and it was my turn to stay with her in the way mothers and children do in generations of our family. And I never got there and worse I never let her know I was coming. Outside her bay window are the mountain totara and the purple azalea she chose for their uniqueness.

Now I am winging home in the aeroplane. I am minding the two nikau seedlings from the treeman to plant for her in Auckland. My heart gasps at the nor'west arch of fiery scarlet, the wine rainbow, the warm wind blowing the temperate air.

Note: 'High Country Weather', from Baxter, James K., *Collected Poems*, ed. J. E. Weir (Oxford University Press, 1979), reproduced with permission.

Discovery at Canterbury Museum

Siobhan Harvey

As the cancer morphined your body into a mummy,
I retreated to the Museum. There, I lingered
before the taxidermic welcome of the Discovery Room,
strayed into the Fossil Dig and spidered my way
through the Star-dome which spun a heavenly elegy
from the Southern Hemisphere night sky.

A creepy-crawly koru, swirled from the Bug Wall's
metamorphosed insects, offered further hope.
But it was the crocodile, Plutarch's Divine Logos
which, blackened by atrophy and strapped to a stretcher
above my head, led me to see beyond an end to things;
and so I fled – out, out towards the exit,
where images from a snowflake exhibition
floated, like angels, up towards the heavens.

First published in *The Listener*, September 2007

One Christchurch Evening

Michael Hall

Near the hotel
a gull on a streetlamp
to almost 20 years
now
has lost his summer

a memorial arch
hides the interior
moment
a bookstore closing

for the evening
a young woman's thoughts
at a bus stop
down Worcester Street

you cannot see them
only her,
the others that blur by
and the cathedral

tolls, a little piece
a cold jigsaw sound for a city
once home and of varsity,
now as if bought in a second hand
shop

pieces missing.
Hagley's losing leaves.

The city this evening has bright arms
in the April fog
its suburbs a cardigan
of malls

and takeaways.
That young woman

I remember.

Going to the Pictures 1953

Annie Orre

Creative nonfiction

My mother took me often to the movies. We said we were going to the 'pictures' or the 'flicks'. We'd get there on the No. 6 bus cocooned in the smoky air, as passengers puffed on their cigarettes and ground out the butts on the linoleum-covered floor.

> I gaze out the windows
> go faster bus
> transport me

At the Avon Theatre in Worcester Street, my mother pays for the back stalls, 2/9 with me half price. The seats are worn; a thousand bottoms have wriggled here watching the flicks. People have wiped away tears in the dark, so no-one will see, and laughed belly shrieks that echoed through the high ceiling and glassy dome.

> the lights are dimmed
> we stand
> for God Save the Queen

The velvet curtains swish aside; a large white screen displays advertisements of men on horses lighting up Pall Malls, enticing us with their sophistication, and of children licking Tip Top ice cream cones, and I whine to Mum that I want to see the film and why should we endure all this rubbish? The shorts are shown first, a newsreel of the world news in black and white, accompanied by a posh BBC voice; he sounds breathless and excited at the same time. A Popeye cartoon contrasts.

> loud music startles
> the MGM lion rolls
> his head, roars

I am transfixed, in the dark; the scent of Evening in Paris wafts from my mother. She opens her handbag, pulls out a bag of Minties. As we suck, I am absorbed in *Roman Holiday* with Audrey Hepburn and Gregory Peck. Audrey Hepburn is Princess Ann and she falls in love with Gregory Peck as they whiz around Rome on a Vespa. I am Audrey Hepburn, there in the dark, smile like her, tap my feet to the music. My mother nudges me, whispers to keep still. We hold sticky hands.

> the lights come on at interval
> pale on the screen
> 'Time for a Capstan'

I buy a frozen ice cream in the foyer, near the ticket seller who slumps in her glassed-in booth. I tell Mum when I grow up I want to be a film star and wear glamorous dresses and high heels. If I can't be a film star, I'd like to own a picture theatre and go to every show. My mother nods and smiles; her brown curls bob up and down.

> the matinee is over
> home, yawning on the bus
> next week we'll go again to Hollywood

Sonnet on the # 10 Bus

Marisa Cappetta

Port Hills is a
prosaic walk in
a name she said
yours is written
she squinted along
her finger tracing
cursive script
in the air
the inscription
on brown tussock

hills claims me
a string attached
reels me in every
night by red bus

First published in *Takahe* 64, August 2008

Lights Out on the City that Shines

Doc Drumheller

On the 150th
year celebration
of Christchurch
grey clouds rolled in
from the hills.

Goth teenagers
huddled together
in Cashel Mall,
penguins waddled
in from the Antarctic.

Japanese children
dressed as sheep
bounced in harnesses,
bearded wolves
took photographs.

The Mayor carved up
a 150 foot
birthday cake
in a garden
of hawthorn berries.

One man dances
to the covers band
as hundreds line up
to have their smiles
painted on.

Christchurch Gothic

David Eggleton

Summer's Avon spelt the names of atua in green,
and through trees sun shafts dug at dappled lawns,
as if to unearth a circuit-board of worm-holes,
the universe beneath the labyrinth,
the silent presence of mountain shingle
across the curve of the island's waist.

Teen racers hummed like bees in a hive,
and late autumn was the harlequin
hurrying past them down Bealey Ave,
towards the rusted, busted, midnight hour,
its sword-and-sorcery pageant of flashing sabres,
its chorus lines of black on moonlit runnelled iron.

They drained the swamp for bodies,
and found a city in a smog overcoat the colour
of mid-winter: a swallowed-up netherland.
Around it, paddock windbreaks rose in ranks,
long shadows falling like guillotines,
as night exhaled its nausea.

Frosted spring melted into this deep carpet,
and from Port Hills rolled the squared-away harvest,
whose matted roots expressed pedigrees of settlement,
a holding pattern of heartbeats, brainwaves, fingerprints
down blind alleys. The city breathed in —
a hot air balloon sailed above its festoons of bitumen.

Night Creatures

Laurence Fearnley

A memoir

Looking back, the Port Hills were far more removed from the city of Christchurch in the early 1970s than they are now. There were tracks and scenic view points, but once darkness fell the Summit Road was more or less deserted. Now, when I travel its length I'm aware of cars, mountain cyclists, day walkers and buildings disrupting my view – or rather, my image of how things used to be. A gondola ferries visitors to the top of Mt Caversham and, from there, I can look across the valley towards brightly coloured paragliders floating and spiralling towards Heathcote Valley. I can measure the slow progress of dog walkers and joggers zig-zagging their way up the Bridle track, or I can fix my gaze on the conveyor belt of gondola pods – some full, many empty, as they lurch to and fro, on their short journey to the hilltop station. At night, the road is no longer silent. Broken bottles, tyre-marked 'doughnuts' in parking areas illustrate the level of activity which takes place after dark.

There was a period during my early childhood when the Summit Road was all but silent after dark. Mid-week, during term time, my parents would take us – my brother and myself – to the Port Hills where we would sleep, returning to the city early the following morning.

I never understood how the decision was reached to leave our house in the suburb of Shirley and follow the long avenue through Linwood before winding up the hillside of Mt Pleasant to the Summit Road. I have no recollection of any family discussion ever having taken place. What I do remember is that sometimes my father would arrive home from work in the evening and, perhaps sensitive to the way the light was falling through the trees surrounding our garden, would look at my mother and, wordlessly, through a slight gesture which only my mother understood, ask, 'What do you think?' Or maybe my mother, going into the garden to fetch the washing, would notice how much warmer the air was outside than inside our gloomy two-storeyed home. As she reached for the clothes which hung, warm and stiff on the line, she may have hesitated, and murmured to herself, 'What a beautiful evening. It would be good to watch the sun set, don't you think?' If a question ever did exist, then my parents must have answered, 'Yes, why not?'

Whatever the prompt, we would find ourselves gathering our sleeping bags and then, within minutes, we would pull our solid front door closed behind us as we headed out into a warmer, lighter, carefree world. Even as a five- or six-year-old, I was conscious of a sense of anticipation and freedom – a state that I am transported back to whenever I happen to sleep rough.

With the sun low in the sky, we would squeeze through the wires in the fence and meander through tussocks, past grazing sheep before spotting a rocky outcrop near the top of a hill. Facing west, we could look across the plains towards the Alps and, there, on a patch of tufted grass sheltered from the wind, we would lay out our sleeping bags. For something so simple, it was incredibly thrilling.

It never occurred to me that what we were doing was as foreign to my parents' own childhood as it was unheard of among my school friends. I knew no one in my class made these mid-week outings – but, for some reason, it didn't cross my mind that spending a night sleeping out was something that my parents hadn't experienced as children. It all seemed so natural – such a part of them – that I guess I thought they'd grown up in England doing what we did. In reality, at an age when I was camping, mucking about looking for skinks, my mother was likely to have been stuck in a tiny air raid shelter in the bottom of her garden. My father, on the other hand, had been evacuated during the war – sent off to a small Catholic town in Ireland, where, for as long as he remained, he was singled out and bullied as a Protestant. How he dealt with his experiences remains as much a mystery now as it was then.

However, I think the main reason we were taken away to sleep under the stars was simply because it was something my parents wanted to do. It wasn't something that they did for us – in the way that we fuss around with our kids now, explaining in prissy voices that we want to 'give them experiences' – it was something they did for themselves, for pleasure. They were, in effect, making up for lost time and so if they wanted to spend a school night sleeping out on a hillside, we did.

In Christchurch a nor'west evening can be very beautiful. Though buffeting and aggravating during the day, often by sunset the wind relaxes, becoming a soft warm breeze – one that strokes the tussocks like an invisible hand. Looking across the plains, you can see the remarkable arc of cloud which seems to run the entire length of the Alps. Below this arc is blue sky and, occasionally, the small black dot of an aeroplane drifting into view. As the light falls, you can make out the blinking lights of these planes, just as you become increasingly aware of the gold and orange city lights below. But more thrilling than any of these 'man-made' lights is the single sparkle of Venus; way off to the west, visible just after sunset, when the sky is tinged green.

Above all, these evenings in a tent were peaceful and sensory, a simple enjoyment or appreciation of being outside. We didn't have to do anything – we had eaten at home – we just had to settle into the warmth of our sleeping bags and pass the time until morning. Lying in a sleeping bag, enjoying the remains of the day; the problem was not how to fall asleep but, rather, how to stay awake. The very idea of sleeping – of missing out on all that was going on – was absurd. I would be very aware of my father's snoring long before I succumbed to sleep myself.

From experience, I had learnt that one of the best ways to keep awake was by talking aloud to myself. And so I would begin; mumbling my way through a rambling, fragmented monologue, a speech that listed everything I had seen or done since arriving. As lists go, it was very detailed. If I began by describing a skink my father had shown me, I would tease the image out until I had satisfied myself that I had not only a true and accurate description of the skink, but of the rock on which it was found, the lichen on the rock, the grass beside the rock, the sheep droppings on the grass – whether they were round, marble like, or larger yam-like specimens. I would remember the sheep; their numbers, how they grazed, whether or not they made a sound as they cropped the grass, whether or not they ran away or stood watching as we approached. Having taken care of the flora and fauna I would have to sit up and look at the city lights – did they shimmer? Did they resemble stars or were they sparkly – like the sun reflecting on water? Could I trace my way back to our house via Linwood Avenue – a long, straight road that cut a path from the dark void of the estuary to the thread of black, which was the Avon River? On and on, I mumbled. Was that an aeroplane or a satellite? Star or a planet? Orion? And this is where I usually came unstuck – I had no idea. But what I was looking at was remarkable and therefore I just had to tell my parents about it. There was nothing subtle about my method in regard to stirring them awake. In fact, I doubt they were asleep. In all likelihood they would have been listening, gritting their teeth, keeping quiet for fear of encouraging me.

I can imagine it: the what's that, whatsthat, wasssthat? as I tried to prolong the conversation, needing more than the monosyllabic answers 'aeroplane,' 'Lancaster Park,' 'ship' to my increasingly scattered questions. Though I drove them insane, my parents never snapped at me. They might ignore me, but they never told me to shut up and go to sleep.

Eventually, however, I would drift off. I think it was the combination of feeling the warm breeze across my face, hearing its gentle gusts as it teased the tussocks – but also the slight dampness as dew formed on my sleeping bag – and most gentle of all, the sound of sheep baaing softly in the night. I loved – still love – the presence of night creatures, even if they are just sheep. There is, to my mind, nothing quite so soothing or calming as being in a world surrounded by animals or birds when sleeping out at night. In all senses, it is a manifestation of the peaceable kingdom made all the more comforting by hearing the soft sound of my father's voice, whispering, 'Night and Bless,' as if to the stars.

I doubt there's a child alive who wants to fall asleep under such conditions.

Note: An extract from *Campsites: a memoir about tents*, a work in progress.

Castle Rock

Helen Lowe

Rotating in mid-air,
suspended between blue above,
bleached tussock below,
face to face with the ragged crag
of Castle Rock, sun flashes
off her watch, dazzling
as the first time they met
in the Roxborough fish and chip
shop, high above the Clutha River:
his presence, blazing in,
was like the sun rising,
spilling over energy, snaring her
with his eagerness for living –
dazzled then too, but now
her eyes clear, take in hill, sky,
rock, as someone shouts – she kicks
hard into the face, finds purchase
as the rope plays out.

First published in *The Press*, Christchurch, July 2007.

Haast Amongst the Moa

David Eggleton

Mountains are your eagle claws,
your aquiline beak.
Maverick feathery prey in tussock,
swamp or sandhill,
they were dug from a bog.
Now home is a hollow log
in a museum diorama,
while the billy boils.
The taxidermied crowd regards you
with glass eyes.
Muscular Christians,
whole mustering gangs,
have gone the way of all flesh.
A kea's scream rattles down scree
and up hawk spurs;
a greenstone mere thrills to the marrow.
Wrestling with a taniwha,
on a turbulent riverbed;
eels of water welling from a bore,
as rata bloom maps the province in red.

First published in *The Press*, Christchurch, February 2009

Sculptress Wife of a Hero

Nancy Cawley

Kathleen Scott sculpted the marble monument to her husband, Antarctic explorer Captain Robert Falcon Scott, which stands beside the Avon River in Worcester Street, Christchurch.

After her husband's death, she continued sculpting the important men of her time. Many of them, it has been suggested, fell in love with her. On 24 July 1947, she died of leukaemia in England, aged 69, choosing as her epitaph: Kathleen. No happier woman ever lived.

Kathleen Bruce was born in 1878. She was the youngest of a family of 11 which included two sets of twins. Her father was a small-time parson, her mother a cousin of Lord Elgin, descended from an emperor of Constantinople, whose wife is said to have brought as part of her dowry a small fishing village, now known as Venice.

Perhaps Kathleen Bruce's strengths came from weathering misfortunes. Her mother became blind at her birth and died a year later, at the age of 42. Her unhappy father remarried, unsuccessfully, and died when she was seven. It was left to a wealthy academic, great-uncle William Skene, of Edinburgh, to provide the Bruce tribe with a home and upbringing. In a biography of Kathleen, *A Great Task of Happiness* (1995), her grand-daughter, Louisa Young, describes the children as being ostensibly well brought up, but really 'a bunch of little monkeys.' 'The Bruces were very much a Victorian family: huge, resilient, religious, stiff upper lipped, and with a streak of eccentricity,' writes Louisa Young. Kathleen Bruce added substantially to the last trait. From boarding school, an elder Bruce sister wrote, 'Naughty little Kathleen is always in hot water.'

By the time she was 20, Kathleen had settled down a little. She was channelling her passion for life into a course at the Slade art school in London. She studied drawing, painting and modelling in clay. In Paris she met Picasso and studied with Rodin.

In 1900, with her studies completed, the young sculptress travelled widely in Europe. She called it 'vagabonding'. She did relief work in Macedonia, delivered the baby of Isadora Duncan in a hideaway in the Netherlands, trekked through Italy with a male artist friend in borrowed peasant clothes, and slept alone on Greek hillsides. In Turkey, in a room where rats scampered at night, she battled through typhoid.

Kathleen was widely admired and courted by men. Her friends included George Bernard Shaw, Aubrey Beardsley, T.E. Lawrence and Norwegian explorer, Fridtjof Nansen. Lovers came and went. The wife of one took poison but survived.

Kathleen Bruce was 29 when she met Robert Falcon Scott at a London tea-party. Shy and reserved, the young naval officer was 10 years older than Kathleen. He had led his first Antarctic expedition three years earlier. Kathleen found herself balancing a cup of tea and, as she later wrote, 'being trivially chaffed by this very well-dressed, rather ugly and celebrated explorer'. She noted his 'rare smile and eyes of a quite unusual dark blue, almost purple. He suggested taking me home'.

In 1908, Kathleen and her 'Con' were married by royal permission in the Chapel Royal at Hampton Court. Auguste Rodin and his wife were among the 150 guests; the King sent a telegram. The Scotts' only child, Peter, was born a year later.

When Scott and his men sailed from Lyttelton in the *Terra Nova* on 29 November 1910, on his second trip to the Antarctic, he and Kathleen had two busy years of marriage behind them. With the wives of other officers, Kathleen farewelled the expedition at the port, but wrote afterwards, 'I didn't say good-bye to my man because I didn't want anyone to see him sad.' She never saw him again.

In the summer of 1913, Kathleen Scott was on a boat in the Pacific, on her way to welcome the expedition back, when she learned via a wireless message that her husband and his companions had died of starvation and scurvy on the way back from the South Pole. It had happened more than a year earlier.

In New Zealand, surviving members of the expedition gave Scott's widow his letters and diary. Kathleen felt admiration as well as love for her explorer husband. She wrote, 'There never was a man with such a sense of responsibility and duty, and the agony of leaving his job undone, losing the other lives, and leaving me uncared for must have been unspeakable.' Expedition members buried Scott and his men under a snow cairn and raised crossed skis above them. Louisa Young writes in her book, 'The bodies are no longer there: the movement of the ice will have brought them gradually north. In about 1985, their cairn will have broken off as an iceberg, sending them out into the Antarctic seas like a frozen Viking burial'.

Kathleen Scott married Edward Hilton in 1922, 11 years after Scott's death, when she was 43. Later Hilton was made a British cabinet minister, and became Lord Kennet. Their son, Wayland, had six children – including Louisa Young.

The year after Scott's death, a Christchurch committee commissioned a commemorative statue. The thousand pound fee was raised by public appeal. The 42-tonne four-metre-high monument was shipped free from London and unveiled on its present site in 1917. A bronze replica stands in London's Wellington Place. Two sections of the Christchurch statue remain rough and unfinished – a hand and a leg support, left in this state for strength in transit. Kathleen Scott was to have revisited New Zealand to complete the work, but World War I intervened and the trip was never made.

The bronze plaque on the base of the statue carries the well-known words from Captain Scott's diary: 'I do not regret this journey, which shows that Englishmen can endure hardships, help one another and meet death with as great a fortitude as ever in the past'.

First published in *The Press*, Christchurch, 1997

A Book on Birds

kimbala

Evening in the Botanical Gardens.
The information centre is closed.
Shat-spat twigs
whiten to grey
in the fat summer light.

A bird-woman came here once.
She opened her cloaks wide and a nesting pair
of every sort of bird fell to the floor.
The Cormorants flew to the trees above the lake
and made of their horny mess
giant nests
of fur balls and great tangles
of lichen green wool.
Composed for her
scribbled and goaded into all the available
crooks and elbows of branches.

A couple of good old blokes walk by the lake
'Birds – you say?'
'Yeah – well I,
I've got a book on birds.
It's got *Playboy* on the front.'

An Old Maroon

Sara Newman

A memoir

An oak tree that is not; a Clayton's oak. I passed it in the morning as I crossed the park and idly thought 'beech', not knowing that it was called an oak tree, until one day I stopped to read the inscription on the brass plaque beneath it:

Known as the 'lone oak'
this beech tree marks
the practice grounds
used for many years by
University of Canterbury Rugby Players
Old Maroons Assoc.
Nov. 1994

On winter mornings a silver path arrows across the frosty grass and passes close by the old tree. I look towards the playing field and imagine those young men at early morning practice tossing the rugby ball to each other. I see their breath white against the grey mist which hides the trunks of tall pines, their giant heads silhouetted in space. I smile to think that the flower of Canterbury's young intellectuals called that beech a lone oak.

In spring the sun lights up its young leaves with green energy. I remember my brother, David, an Old Maroon, wearing the maroon rugby jersey with its white collar. He played representative rugby for Canterbury University in 1939 and proudly wore the Maroon's shield with its Golden Fleece, wheat sheaves, plough, oval ball and goal posts. He was a clever boy and, when he finished high school, left the farm to train as a teacher.

The bluestone, neo-Gothic Teachers' Training College, west of Cranmer Square, has long since been turned into luxury apartments. The 1863 wooden building which housed the tuck shop, looking as if it had escaped from toy town, still stands on the corner of Montreal and Kilmore Streets. The old university campus is now the Art Centre. Canterbury was the university that gathered up country boys from around the South Island and gave them space to grow.

I can see my brother now in my mind's eye, wearing a dust-covered worn leather jacket, goggles and leather gloves, cresting the last small hill on our drive astride his motor bike, arriving home to a hero's welcome from one young sister. He rode up from Christchurch, stopping at farms along the way through North Canterbury, offering to do labouring jobs to help pay his way through university.

'Hoeing swedes is a killer. My arms are ready to drop off by the end of the day,' he said. 'But weeding onions is the worst.' He was tanned and honed. Once home, it was back to work on our farm till the vacation was over. Those early Canterbury students were in touch with the wheat sheaves, fleece and plough on the University's heraldic shield.

In 1939 Britain declared war on Germany. Prime Minister Savage said to the people of New Zealand, 'When Britain is in trouble, we are in trouble and where she goes, we go: where she stands, we stand …' and they did, because that was how New Zealand was then; that was the sentiment of our own first generation New Zealand family; those were the days when we stood to sing 'God Save the Queen' before the film started in the picture theatre.

On 3 September 1939, New Zealand independently declared war on Germany.

On 15 September David rode off to enlist and swear 'to bear true allegiance to our sovereign Lord, the King'. He chose to join the Engineering Corps because his father had served as an engineer in the Great War. He and his friend claimed the dubious honour of being the first names on the Canterbury list: 'four figure' men, so called because later echelons had longer numbers. They misrepresented their ages, putting them forward two years. It felt like a great lark, and they laughed at the thought of wearing the khaki lemon squeezer and slapped each other on the shoulders as they left the registry. David claimed to be twenty-one and born two years before his parents met. No doubt his Lord, the King, had more important things on his mind than checking the birth dates of lowly recruits.

David trained at Burnham Military Camp. Then there was the dreaded final leave.

I remember that final leave; our mother fussing over David, doing things for him that didn't need to be done, re-pressing his battle jacket with tears splashing on the coarse khaki pocket. I remember our father standing with his shoulders straighter than usual talking ordinary talk, but glancing sideways at his son when he thought no one was watching.

Young men on final leave had one week at home before they left for the theatre of war, as it was called. Some days in that week seemed endless and some had wings, until suddenly it was all over. The hand-made hussif from the Country Women's Institute, given at the farewell dance on the last night at home, was packed in his kit bag, and David was gone. He sailed to Africa with the first echelon on 4 January 1940 and disembarked in Egypt on 13 February; he was transformed in six months from a nineteen-year-old student to a twenty-one-year-old fighting soldier.

David's actual 21st birthday was celebrated in Stalag 18A. He had been taken prisoner of war.

'It was Anzac Day, 25 April 1941,' he told me, 'and we had already lost many men. All around us red poppies flowered in the fields and we knew then their real significance and, probably for the first time, all that was meant by Anzac Day. Before the day was over we were completely broken up by the ferocity of the German air and land attack and those who were not killed were taken prisoner. God, it was dreadful; it was humiliating. It crushed out of us all the pride we had built to keep us going.'

The engineers were detailed to cover the retreat across the bridge over the Corinth Canal. The Germans were known to be advancing so the main body of men was ordered to cross the bridge and retreat down the Greek Peninsula. Five engineers were to cross the bridge last and blow it up before the Germans could follow. The retreat was going according to plan when suddenly the sky was filled with German parachutes. The bridge blew up before the men could cross. It may have slowed the enemy advance through Greece; some historians believe it was the first turning point of the War.

The surrounding ground was flat with small mogul-bumps and hollows and scattered sparingly with matagouri-like scrubby bushes. There was nowhere to hide.

'It was those scrubby bushes, the feel of Canterbury high country; that Canterbury ochre,' David told me, 'that made me think of home.'

He had not felt it before; the 'left, right, left, right' discipline was designed to kill emotion. He was one of three who survived and were taken prisoner.

'What was it like?' I asked years later.

'I learned to sing "Lili Marlene" in German.'

'What were the Germans like?'

'Well, I remember my birthday, my twenty-first. We were mixing concrete in an industrial camp, doing building work on a huge hydro-electric plant at Lavamund. At the time we were walking round and round a central pole in a large tank, pushing a heavy, wooden arm which turned a paddle in the mix. We were covered in water and cement and ordered to push till we fell. When that happened our place was taken by another prisoner. One of the guards, who liked to practise his English, said as I passed him, "Hello, soldier, how are you?" I said, "It's my twenty-first birthday." He waited till I fell off the next time, called me out of the crew and beckoned for me to follow him into the lea of the vats where we were out of the wind. He gave me the last half of his cigarette. "Happy birthday," he said in English.'

David was finally discharged from the army in April 1946. He returned home later than most because he had escaped prison camp and fought with Marshall Tito's men in Yugoslavia for the last years of the war. It was to England that the Bristol Freighter flew him and he returned later to march past Buckingham Palace in the Victory Parade.

He came back to Canterbury with the handsome gratuity of £273 12s 2d for his six years' army service.

David turned from the plough, wheat and fleece of Canterbury to the heraldic book of learning, completed his degree and worked around the environs of the Province before his career took him north to Auckland. It was a life story similar to that of many young men who grew up in Canterbury in the 1930s. Tough and strong, those men came back from the war and rebuilt their lives. They knew the brilliant colour of an autumn harvest reaped from Canterbury seed.

The Glove

Lois Farrow

Creative nonfiction

Why was it him, not me, I agonised. No one would have missed me. But Paul! Paul had a wife and gorgeous young daughter. Why him?

I was just a young fellow then, fresh out of university and bursting with energy. Our accounting firm was the best in Christchurch: F.C. BROWN & ASSOCIATES. The name was displayed above our modest offices in Armagh Street. Each day I would catch the tram into town, climb the stairs and settle into work. Figures always fascinated me. I could add up the columns faster than anyone in the office.

'It's your young brain, Matthew,' F.C. used to tell me. 'Keep it active boy, and you'll do well.' Old F.C. was good to us young fellows. He had a good brain in his head, too, in spite of not much covering on top; his hair was all on his upper lip, shaped grandly into a flowing moustache. Clients always had a smile when they left his office. His kindly manner set them at ease as he unravelled the intricacies of their accounts. I aspired to be like him.

One of the associates was Thomas Blackburn. A bit younger than Old F.C., Thomas was a dapper little man. His suit was dry-cleaned every week, although it never really got dirty, not in an accountants' office. His wife sent him to work with a clean shirt every day, and the decorative hanky peeking out of his top pocket would always match his tie. Nice man, Thomas, gentlemanly and discreet, and very helpful.

Thomas didn't always know how to take Paul and me. We were the youngest in the office and brought life into the place, Paul always said, so it wasn't too staid and stuffy. Mrs. Mitchell, the typist, liked to say, 'Tut, tut, young fellows, what will you do next?' but she loved laughing at Paul's jokes. And did she make a fuss when Paul's wife, Millie, brought the baby in? Little Sarah was six months old at that time and would smile at everyone. Aw, I didn't know anything about babies, but even I could see she was a cute little thing. And Mrs. Mitchell, well, you'd have thought she was the grandmother the way she went on. Paul had been in the office for five years, and Mrs. Mitchell had a real soft spot for him and Millie, and now for the baby.

Mostly we worked in our own office, but at audit time we would be sent to the client. That was always good; gave a bit of variety. This time we were working at Ballantynes on Cashel Street. Their audit was one of our biggest, and it was taking several weeks, even though there were three of us on the job: Thomas, Paul and me. Unlike our previous job, where the offices were light and airy with plenty of windows, the room they gave us at Ballantynes was a poky one: an inside room with no windows, lit by artificial light. It was a bit hard on the eyes, but we got used to it, and the chaps were good to work with. Paul and me, we always made sure each day was a good one. Another week and we'd be finished.

On Monday night 17th November, Old F.C. rang me at home.

'Matthew, there's an urgent job come up in Papanui,' he said. 'Will you go there tomorrow, son, and see to it? You should get it done in one day, and then you can get back to Ballantynes.'

Well, of course, you don't say no to the boss. So the next day I went to Papanui to sort that little job out. It was a nice day with summer just around the corner and in my lunch time I sat outside by the fountain. As I was eating my tomato and cucumber sandwiches, who should come along but Paul's wife, Millie, with little Sarah in the carriage. Nice to see a familiar face, and Sarah was all smiles as usual. We chatted for a bit then they carried on. She had a busy day, Millie said, getting ready for Paul's birthday later that week.

After they'd gone, I saw the little pink glove on the ground. That's Sarah's, I thought, picking it up. I looked, but Millie was nowhere in sight; it was too late to run after them. I put it in my pocket; I would give it to Paul tomorrow.

About four the job was finished so I left to go home. As I went outside and waited for the tram, I looked towards the city. A huge pall of smoke hung in the air. Wonder what's happening there, I thought.

It wasn't till later that evening I heard the news of Ballantynes' fire. Thomas and Paul in their inner room had no chance at all.

I looked at the little pink glove in my hand. Why was it him, I wondered, and not me?

Note: All names in this story have been changed.

Hopton 'Barker' Rediscovered

Jenny Haworth

Lady Barker, well-known internationally for her books, Station Life in New Zealand *and* Station Amusements in New Zealand, *arrived pregnant in Lyttelton in October 1865. She had married Frederick Broome in 1865 after her first husband, George Barker, died of fever in India in 1861; Barker had been knighted for services during the Indian Mutiny.*

Lady Barker's new husband had been farming in New Zealand since he was 15 years old and he had returned to buy a sheep station, Broomielaw, on the banks of the Selwyn River. When the Barkers arrived their new house was not ready and so Lady Barker stayed in Christchurch where her son, Hopton, was born. Not long after, she moved from the boarding house where she was living to stay at Ilam, the home of the Watts-Russells. It was here that young Hopton became ill with infant diarrhoea. The local doctor, James Turnbull, blamed the nor'wester for the illness and advised them to leave Christchurch for Broomielaw even though their new home was far from ready.

For a while Hopton rallied; 'the weather was exquisitely bright and sunny and yet bracing. Baby was to be kept in the open air as much as possible and so F−− and I spent our days on the downs near the house, carrying our treasure by turns.' But the diarrhoea returned and after a violent attack Hopton 'was taken to the land where pain is unknown.'

In her letter (IX) Lady Barker describes his death: 'During the last twelve hours of his life, as I sat before the fire with him on my lap, poor F−− kneeling in perfect agony of grief by my side, my greatest comfort was in looking at that exquisite photograph from Kehren's picture of the 'Good Shepherd'. For Lady Barker, comfort came from the face of Christ who was 'portrayed as one of intense feminine compassion and tenderness that it makes me feel more vividly, "In all our Sorrows He is afflicted".'

According to Betty Gilderdale, author of *The Seven Lives of Lady Barker*, Frederick Broome was sent to Christchurch to summon the doctor, but he arrived too late. The baby was brought back and buried in the Barbados Street Cemetery. No permanent headstone was ever raised over the grave, and with time its place was forgotten.

Recently Hopton Napier Broome's grave has been rediscovered in Christchurch's historic cemetery. His was one of numerous unmarked graves but interest in his mother prompted attempts to rediscover it. As Lady Barker, she was well-known to New Zealanders for her lively, evocative accounts of life on a Canterbury sheep station in the late 1860s. Her first book, *Station Life in New Zealand*, was published in 1870 after her return to Britain. It was based on letters that she wrote to her sister, Louisa Scott, and on her diaries. The book was an instant success and was translated into French and German. The sequel, *Station Amusements in New Zealand*, followed in 1873.

The rediscovery of the grave is the work of Bede Cosgriff. He got maps of the cemetery from the Council and found that there were not one but two Broome plots and neither of them was marked with a visible plaque. With City Council help, a ground penetrating radar (GPR) was used to locate the child's grave. Peter Sheild of Radar Investigations carried out a survey on 3 November 2005. In his report he wrote: 'A Noggin 250 Smartcart GPR was used … Strong sub-surface detail was revealed to a depth of 2.5 metres … The depth of the grave was approximately 1.2 metres.' What he had found was the remains of the baby – Hopton Napier Broome.

For Bede, locating the grave and getting the plaque installed was a recognition of Lady Barker and her importance in telling the story of life in early Canterbury. She was 'a great publicist for New Zealand and Canterbury,' he said. 'With her zest and enthusiastic writing she gave many people in Britain knowledge of what life was like here.'

Previously published in *Heritage New Zealand*, the magazine of the New Zealand Historic Places Trust.

Note on Names: Lady Barker did come to New Zealand as Mrs Broome. The birth of Hopton was recorded in the *Press* as 'to the wife of F.N. Broome a son.' But it was socially acceptable for titled women in the 19th century to retain their titles and name if they married again. Also their cadet, T.E. Upton, wrote in 1866, 'I forgot to tell you, Mrs Broome has taken her title again on account of some prize money in India.' For the impecunious Broomes, the money was a great help, but one of the conditions under which she received it was that she retain her former husband's name.

Oriana

Bernadette Hall

Ursula you dear,
I loved that peep of you just before we sailed.

No-one else seems to know about the letter.
It's handwritten, wrapped up in white tissue paper
in a manila folder in the Macmillan Brown Library.
It's from Oriana Wilson, Edward's wife.
It's all about the ponies
                              'how I'd love to show them to you'
and New Zealand
                      'how I'd love to live there'
and Christchurch
                        'how I'd love to buy a house near you.'
and a trip she and Ursula had made together
to the Franz Josef glacier.

The day is there, Sunday 27 November, but not the place
or the year. Given the reference to the ponies
and the upside-down stamp of the world with Antarctica
at the top and a little penguin, it's got to be Lyttleton, 1910.

A few nights earlier there'd been a big fight, Mrs Evans
and Mrs Scott slugging it out in the foyer of Warner's Hotel.
'There was more blood and hair flying about
than you would see in a Chicago slaughterhouse in a month,'
wrote Titus Oates who much preferred dogs and horses.

Ory wasn't a bit like that.

When the bad news came through, she burnt all Edward's
letters to protect him from the nosey but she kept the green book.
It was lying open on her husband's chest in the fatal tent,

the pages bruised with ice and wet, 'In Memoriam', by Tennyson.
He'd borrowed it from Cherry-Garrard for the final push south.
For the sake of the words, he'd risked the weight. In 1945,
just before she died, she gave the book back with her thanks.

Note: the Ursula referred to is Ursula Bethell, the celebrated Canterbury poet.

Bernadette Hall: *The Ponies* (Victoria University Press, 2007)

On the Beach

Maggie Belcher

Creative non-fiction

The beach in the early morning has a mellow autumnal glow and is empty save for a group of white figures engaged in martial arts. There are the sand, the rock, the sea and the estuary streaming in from behind the rock. Everything is still; even the sea has ceased its lapping of the night and now lies in perfect calm awaiting the baptism which will occur soon in its waters. Everything is warmed by the sun. The child of the parish is quietly fossicking around the slabs of rock beneath Cave Rock screening the rock pools. The white figures thrust arms and legs into the air, intersecting it – but quietly.

People from the Parish of The Church of the Ascension are drifting down to the beach and gathering in small groups. One woman brings her dog, who looks well in the sun: coffee and cream and shining. He knows it is Sunday and wonders why they are not parked up on the hill at the church. There has never been a departure from plan like this. The church warden is waving a gold liturgy book and a stick aloft, in an effort to assemble people in the shadow of the rock. They continue to drift like seagulls, exclaiming about the sun.

'Look at the sun.'

'Isn't it warm.'

'Good job it wasn't yesterday ... freezing weather ... the sea would have been so cold ...'

More people arrive, parking their cars on the road, scrambling down over large rocks left from the last big storm. The tea-pot and tiara children arrive (they like to wear odd things on their heads for church) and also some elegant parishioners dressed for the ten-o'clock service. A young woman rushes from the gathering back to the car for her guitar.

You might wonder at High Anglicans on a beach like latter day hippies singing to a guitar. But they do and they are. Sing. Smile. Look at the sea. Look at their books. Look at each other. Look at the Vicar dressed in white like the martial arts contingent further up the beach. Look at the two white doves that have arrived on the Cave Rock.

The 'Baptee' arrives wearing blue trousers, a blue shirt and red spiky hair. Her husband is carrying a blue towel over his arm. They are both doctors, so they can treat each other if they get chills.

The Vicar summons people and a semi-circle is formed. The young woman with the red hair walks calmly into the sea and waits for the priest to join her. He walks right in in all his robes. Panic flutters through the crowd. Will they shrink? they think; will he have to have new ones? Does he have trousers underneath? Will they ever see the light of day again?

Emmanuel, in shorts, wades in to join them. The priest puts one hand on the head of the young woman and gently pushes her under three times as the 'watchers on the shore' recite from the Baptism liturgy. It's nearly winter, the troops are thinking, safely warm-socked and warm- booted on the shore.

'It's actually not cold,' the young woman with the red hair calls out.

The priest reads from the gold liturgy book, held by the parish assistant whose toes are in the water. Emmanuel stands respectfully to one side of those in the sea.

'Isn't it fitting that he's there in the sea with them? He looks just like a prophet from the Old Testament,' someone says. Those watching can imagine they are standing by the Red Sea waiting for it to be parted, with the river Euphrates flowing strongly by.

The white doves rise briefly from the rock to hang on a current of air.

Gradually the church people move back to their cars and the dog of the parish narrowly avoids being run over.

What Has Become Plain

Marissa Johnpillai

in those days i believed
that my father was flawless
& your archbishop was the famous one.

the point of your cathedral
tippety-tipped with the pomp
of the mitre of the honcho
of the church of england.

but now you're in perspective,
laid out like a patchwork
of redundant toy bunnies,

sparse glitters of hot tin
roofs, your trinkets
scattered across the bed
like waterways.

i imagine the close-ups.
the bullet
is a bicycle.

the diaspora, sheep
wagging their bedraggled
shit-caked butt-flaps behind them.
three fifty bags full & a bangladeshi boy

with tannin on his fingers accidentally leaves
purple thumbprints on the cash.
he hides under the table.

driving back to churchur --- ---
smooth as a satellite --- ---
another young graduate re-arranges

the paragraphs, the latest

whatever at the local
something. decides to revert
to her maiden name for the by-line.

we have begun our descent into
canterbury, i know you
from the north, from the north east,
from the north north east.

i know you by the smudging
of my nose against the sun-
warmed porthole

of this home-coming plane.

Aiko

Ruth Hanover

Fiction

Only my father knows where we are going. Here we will live, here we will be happy, you will see. That is what he tells us. All I know is the name of the street, Hamilton Ave.

We drive away from the airport and I begin work again. My name is Aiko. You pronounce it, 'I-ko'. I worry that they will play with my name. And, there is the shortening of my father's name to Hiro, my mother's to Ellie. It brings discomfort. But I go on. Aiko, call me Aiko.

My father stops the car on Hamilton Ave. We stand there at four in the afternoon in an empty street, empty save for the breeze. Where is everyone? My mother looks down the street with her fingers at the base of her throat. I turn and see that something gathers in the sky above us. It forms clouds and puffs lightly upwards, then drifts. I watch two or three cycles of this, yet cannot shake my confusion. My mother is the first to utter a long sigh and the single word, 'sakura'. I turn to her and smile. We have left the snow for the cherry blossom.

My mother, Ellie, speaks. 'A street full of cherry blossom trees! Such good fortune. And,' she says, 'we have arrived at the moment the blossom flies.' Her fingers catch, tap at her throat, at the little hollow there. My mother turns to my father, Hiro, who stands proudly as if he knew of this moment, could predict, could catch as ephemeral an event as this. I look at his face and see, yes, that he can.

Moving in takes three days. In Hamilton Ave, morning sun comes into my room through French doors, first lighting a green garden out there. I unpack my books and paints. For three days, my mother unpacks our boxes but spends most of her time, it seems to me, in setting up the little shrine, the shelf with its intricate panels and its mirror. My father says, 'We do not need it here.' But my mother smiles and says, 'Perhaps. We shall see.'

I am just so embarrassed. I persuade my mother to put it in the empty room next to mine. She places the shrine there and checks on it every now and then. At least it is not in the lounge. At least no one else will see it. My father laughs at her; it is gentle; and he says, 'One day we will bring you into this century!' But all the same, even as he walks around the house, chuckling about it, he touches all the things that my mother has placed.

At the end of the unpacking, the three days, my mother takes me out into the street to tell me that of all blossom, the cherry is the most evanescent. I turn the word over in my mind and see that it is linked with the memory of last year's blossom and what she told me then. Evanescent; she said it then, too. I already know that cherry blossom clings to the tree for two or three weeks, then it flies. I know this. I just don't feel the same as my mother and I don't use the same word.

But out on Hamilton Ave, my mother is insistent. She reminds me that every year we wonder at the buds that appear on the black wood, reach out to touch the fragile blossom, but dare not. My mother says that cherry blossom flies at the height of our wonder, at the time before a gift is opened, the time before a lover wakes. She says that! I wonder about her. She is so odd, so embarrassing, my mother.

My father, Hiro, comes home with a bike. 'Here, children bike to school.' I tell him I am not a child. I remind him that I turned thirteen two weeks ago, but a bike it is. Out on Hamilton Ave, two girls in short hair bike up and down and turn in fast circles. Aiko, my name is Aiko.

Every night after our meal, my father, my mother and I walk down Hamilton Ave, me thinking of my friends in Japan, and how I would never walk with my parents there. Mostly when we walk these warm summer evenings, there is no one much in the street. There is the letterbox woman of course and the noise of TV and families talking, arguing. On the weekends, there are joggers and more kids on bikes. But we have a friend already, Mrs Harris, the woman who lives in the corner house opposite. She is about the same age as my mother, perhaps older, and at dusk, she walks around her garden with her cat.

Yes, my mother has a friendship with Mrs Harris. Every afternoon, Mrs Harris works in her garden, in her blue overalls. She scrubs the moss from her wall – of course, my mother approves – or waters the clumps of daisies along the street front. My mother watches and buys flowers for the street, too, violets in purple and blue. Mrs Harris brings us vegetables that are either very large or new. She shows me some dark, green leaves that are edible.

All summer, I bike home every day with my new friends, Charlotte, called Charlie because she was supposed to be a boy, although this seems mean, and Jane, who is thin. They both have such short hair that twists and waves, and Jane's is red. Red! It is so beautiful. I look in the mirror and wonder if I should change my hair. Yesterday, I didn't think I should. But today, I don't know ... mine is so long and so straight.

Every day, we throw our bikes under the cherry tree outside my house, get some juice and something to eat, lots, for Charlie is always hungry, and we sit there for ages. They talk fast, so that I miss my friends in Japan.

Every night for ages, for about a week, I have to go to Mrs Harris with soup and rice and all kinds of things, as she is ill. Why doesn't my mother go? Still, I like to make the tray. I put leaves from the cherry tree, in all their colours, on the tray. I remember what my mother says, that we eat with our eyes.

The leaves on the cherry trees have turned as brittle as paper. I show Charlie and Jane, and I am surprised that they have not noticed. I tell them about my street in Tokyo, where the road goes around a cherry tree that is older than anyone who lives there. Charlie doubts a little that what I say is the truth. We lie under the tree and watch as leaves float down towards us. The leaves are piled high and leaf mounds dot the street. We pile leaves over Charlie, until she is almost covered. It is quite childish, but we are happy.

My mother, Ellie, is not happy tonight. She hates the supermarket queue. 'The women either ignore me, or they hear my accent and shout at me, as if I am deaf as well,' she says.

'Give it time, give it time,' says my father.

On a cold Monday, we bike home and see that all the cherry trees have been trimmed. We walk the length of Hamilton Ave, Charlie, Jane and me, and count twenty-eight trees all with their topmost branches cut. The twigs lie like pick-up-sticks, waiting for a game to begin.

After school on the next day, there are a blue tractor and five men in Hamilton Ave. Charlie says the tractor looks as though it belongs in a book. We go back to my house and I show them how to fold an origami crane. I make just one for Mrs Harris, too. I know that if we fold so many cranes, one thousand I think, it will help someone to recover, but my mother says Mrs Harris is almost well already, because of our soup. It could be true.

Three days later, early morning, on the way to school, there is an orange tractor at the end of the street with more men. They have cut three of the cherry trees down. It must be a disease. I am sad all day. Charlie and Jane ask me what is wrong, but when I tell them, they do not understand. Cherry trees do not seem to mean so much to them.

At the end of the day we bike home, Charlie, Jane and me. We have had sport, which I hate. I am just glad to be going home. It is misty, and freezing.

We turn into Hamilton Ave and I look at the stumps of the trees that were cut that morning. The trunks lie cut in rude slabs and are cast all about the stump. I notice, all of a sudden, that it is not just those few trees, no. More have been cut. We throw our bikes down and we walk faster, counting the stumps.

I run ahead in the dusk and I am up to thirteen with my counting. I feel that I am choking. Jane and Charlie run along beside me, right to the end of Hamilton Ave. From Clyde Road to Ilam Road, every cherry blossom tree has been cut down. 'My mother!' The words catch and I run.

I enter our house and it is silent. I walk through the house and find my mother in the little room beside mine. I see that she has lit the shrine. The room is filled with shadow. When I come in, she does not move. She does not greet me. She just continues to kneel and look at the little shrine. I kneel, too, because I do not know what else to do. I sit before the shrine just to be with my mother, but although I am so close, there is so much space between us. It is the same days later, a week even.

Tonight my father comes home late again. He talks quietly to my mother in the room with the shrine and the shadow. He reasons. He explains. I watch them from the door until I see him turn his face and put his forehead to hers.

'Speak to me, Ellie,' he says.

'*All* the trees,' she answers. 'How could they?'

'Yes, yes. I know, Ellie. But it is done,' says my father.

I back away until my father's voice becomes a soft murmur. I go back to my room and touch the things I have placed on my dresser. There is a photo of my best friend in Japan, Minami, in a silver frame. There is a book from Jane that I have not read. There is a crumpled paper crane that Charlie made. I throw myself on the bed. So many things are strange here that I think about Japan. Should I return? It is such a longing that I have, but what I miss now, here, is my mother. While I am truly here, it feels as if my mother is in Japan, for there is so much space between us.

My father comes home late the next night and the next.

I do not see my mother eat.

In daylight, I bike slowly down Hamilton Ave. It is a clear, bright morning. On the top of each stump is an orange cone. They are odd tombstones. At school, I do not talk with Charlie and Jane any more about the trees, or about my mother. I believe they will not understand.

Over the next few days, a machine digs a ditch in Hamilton Ave, from the Clyde Road end. It is for underground power-lines, Mrs Harris says. It becomes wide and deep. And I notice a curious thing, that it is two metres towards the centre of the road, not along the strip of land the cherry trees grew on, nowhere near. Was it futile, cutting the trees? I cannot help but think so.

Day by day, the ditch grows into a culvert, then a deep canal. Wooden bridges have been hurriedly thrown up over it. I see that they have built the bridges flat, unlike the round bridges in Japan. In the rain that comes, the canal floods with muddy water. At night, the workmen hang lanterns on the bridges. Each has a winking eye. Cones stand at either end of the bridges like sentries.

It has just gone five, yet the early winter nights are so dark. There are shouts on the street and I go out to see. In the gloom, a truck moves slowly down Hamilton Ave. Two men pick up the last of the cherry tree wood, shouting for the truck to stop when they have a piece of the trunk or a branch to throw into the back of the truck. Their manner is rough and I cannot stand the way they touch the wood. Mrs Harris calls across the road, 'Aiko! How are you, Aiko?' She crosses the road to stand beside me but I am already moving. I shout at the men in my own language, 'Leave it! Leave it!' I shout again and again. Then I run. I run down Hamilton Ave and nothing will ever stop me.

I wake confused from a dream of running. And a bridge has some kind of significance, but it is unclear. My mother sits close to me and tells me I have had a fever. 'You will be all right now,' she says. I lift my head and reach out to her, but I cannot. She touches my forehead. 'Lie still,' she says. 'It will take time.' She gives me something hot from a small bowl and she takes my hand gently, then with such strength.

I look across the room and there is my father getting up from a chair by the French doors. He holds me, then he sits back there and speaks. 'Mrs Harris came to us and told us you were upset at the truck. Then you ran down the street,' he says. 'But it took so long to find you. In the end, the police found you. You were gone for hours, in winter.' He looks directly into my eyes, catches my look and nods to reinforce what he says. 'This winter is a cold one, Mrs Harris says. So. *Many* hours.' He puts his arms around himself as if he is cold, my father.

'That night, you became ill. For two days, you have had a fever,' says my mother. 'Mrs Harris comes every day. And your friends, Jane and Charlie.' My mother brings me soup and reads to me as she did when I was a child. I feel that my mother is back and that is what I am happy about.

All this time, my father sits in the chair by the French doors. I look through the glass to the cold, green garden. Dusk. 'It will freeze again tonight,' my father says. 'See how cold it is out there?'

There are footsteps on the gritty path into the garden. Someone is coming. I see Charlie's white face peering through the doors.

'Oh! Charlie!' I say. And I think, my friend Charlie. She stands at the door, falters, then as my father opens the French doors, she holds something out to me. 'I brought you a cherry tree,' she says. 'I don't know if it is the right moment...'

'It is,' I tell her. It is perfect. And I see that, as my mother looks at the little tree, she touches the base of her throat and taps lightly.

Charlie stands quite still in the green garden, holding up the tree. At that moment, as if it were in a children's book, the first flakes of snow drift towards the cherry tree. And a word drifts from somewhere, *evanescent*. The moment *is* evanescent.

First published in *Takahe* 64, August 2008

On Day-release

Michael Harlow

In Cathedral Square the city
    is 'going for green'
Festival for Romance, high
    holiday of the body;
freed to it this first day
    of the New Year, coming
down from a chemical hit,
    swirl takes you; inside

    the music on a rip, you
swing. On stage this hip kid
    on a roll, his granny glasses
    black waistcoat and flower
hat, on his guitar solo, 'I'm going
    to Carolina in my mind',
your hands beating the air, trying

    to make sure you say
that everything stays right
    where it is and now, into
his last chorus, a small
    song can sing. His hands
a blur your hair flying on the
    way to Carolina all the way
day-release, and in the park:

    only yesterday your mother
phoned to say the police had picked
    you up, trying to make sure
you said that *there was something*
    out there – throwing yourself
against the bodies of trees.

Michael Harlow: *Cassandra's Daughter* (Auckland University Press 2005)

Kedgeree Meets Kai: Sir John Cracroft Wilson in Cashmere

Julie Wuthnow

Having spent the better part of his career in India as a judge, civilian soldier and debt collector for the East India Company, in 1854 Sir John Cracroft Wilson was in ill health and in need of a sanctuary from the hardships of tropical India. In part, he was in search of a home away from home, an England that was not England itself. But he was also looking for a bit of India that was not quite India.

Cracroft Wilson purchased a valley in the Port Hills in the predominantly English settlement of Canterbury and named his new home the Cashmere Estate, after the scenic Kashmir Valley in India. His evocation of India is not surprising; he had a very long personal history there, and the story of those years reads like a Kipling novel with its tales of heroism, violence and passionate commitment to England's civilising mission. Cracroft Wilson was a hero in the finest Victorian sense of the word, and by 1854 he was thinking of retirement and in search of a suitable location. When he arrived in Canterbury and assessed the valleys and ridges of the Port Hills, he surveyed the landscape in order to see how he could convert it to farm and pasture land. His focus on financial gain was astute; he was particularly preoccupied with the rate of forest growth and the number of animals that could potentially be slaughtered per annum.

But Cracroft Wilson's story is not purely a tale of avarice, and he did not simply replace one field of bounty, India, with another, New Zealand. The way he enacted 'Englishness' at the Cashmere Estate involved an engagement with Indians, Maori and the landscape itself in complex and sometimes contradictory ways. His choice of property on which to found the estate was an unlikely paradise; it was swampland surrounded by tussock-covered ridges and in need of substantial work in order to become productive. Yet fuelled by colonial zeal, Cracroft Wilson reworked and reconstituted the landscape according to his pastoral vision. He drained the swamp and built a homestead for his family with the dozen or so Indian servants he had brought with him to New Zealand, sometimes referred to as 'Wilson's Hindoos'. Yet while

113

he admired 'his' Indians' capacity for work and laboured side by side with them in draining the swamp, the evidence suggests that he did not consider them his equals, as they were not included in his social circle. As for Maori, they didn't present an immediate concern; he reputedly settled on the South Island in part because there were fewer Maori than on the North Island, and the Cashmere Estate was not a place of settlement for Canterbury Ngai Tahu, although there were trails and *mahinga kai* (food-gathering) sites in the general area.

Thus within the space of a few short months Cracroft Wilson had apparently built a homestead in which everything and everyone were in their proper place. Indeed, he was described by some as 'Toryism upon 2 legs'[1]. He returned to India in late 1854 for what was meant to be a short tour of duty before retirement, only to get caught up in the Indian Mutiny of 1857–58. Nonetheless, things appeared to carry on uneventfully in his absence and subsequent to his return in 1859.

Appearances were deceptive, however. While Maori were largely absent from Cashmere Estate in the literal sense, they nonetheless comprised a significant and menacing presence in Cracroft Wilson's imaginings of the future of the New Zealand colony. His views were extreme even at a time when most Europeans believed Maori to be an inferior race, and '[he] stated once that it was "one of the maddest experiments that humanity has ever tried" to attempt to govern, by means of free institutions, a land in which "seven-tenths of the landed gentry were barbarous (sic) savages and three tenths of them were cannibals".'[2] He became a Member of Parliament in 1861, and as he declared in Parliamentary debates that year, at a time when there was open warfare between Maori tribes and English settlers in the North Island, 'We wish to help you; but we will bring you to your senses if you resist Her Majesty's authorities.'[3] The means by which Cracroft Wilson proposed to subdue Maori was once again 'his' Indians, in this case Indian soldiers or 'ghurkas'.

Cracroft Wilson also had a more complex relationship with the Indians at Cashmere than is immediately apparent; they were never simply compliant with his wishes. A number of Wilson's Indian labourers left his employ prior to the expiration of their contracts when they found higher wages elsewhere. They were duly taken to court, in spite of the fact that he gave them land and livestock of their own and granted them independence once their contractual terms had been met. Many found the Canterbury climate unbearably cold; some were sent back to India as a result, and others died. There was a reported death by tutu poisoning (a native shrub), possibly self-inflicted, and reputedly a ghost in the Old Stone House, as a result of jealousy, murder and the disruption of the murdered man's bones in the baker's oven.

At first glance, Cracroft Wilson appears to be almost a caricature of colonial propriety, and he brought to Canterbury a strong vision of paradise that demarcated the proper place of Englishmen, Indians and Maori, as well as a mapping of landscape as primarily an engine of economic prosperity. Yet he repeatedly revealed hints of respect for Indians, an attitude that taints such a purist view. And while Maori were intentionally absent from Cracroft Wilson's estate, they too lurked as a powerful and ever-present threat around the edges of his vision.

Traces of Cracroft Wilson's colonial project persist into the twenty-first century. The homes on the ridge surrounding the original estate are amongst the most affluent in Christchurch, and, as one proceeds downhill towards the valley, residents drive on suburban streets named Shalamar, Bengal and Lucknow, even though the generous boundaries of the original estate have long since been subdivided. The Old Stone House built for 'Wilson's Hindoos' in 1870 still stands, albeit transformed into a community centre.

Sir John has not entirely disappeared.

115

Notes:
1. Rona E. Tolmie, "The political career of Sir John Cracroft Wilson", MA Thesis, University of Canterbury, 1982.
2. Ibid., p. 8.
3. Ibid., p. 18.

Other references:
Betty Roberts & N.F. Roberts, *Old Stone House, 1870–1990 and the Cracroft Community Centre of Christchurch, 1972–1990*, Lincoln, NZ: Te Waihora Press, 1991.
Te Maire Tau, Informal conversation with Dr Tau, member of Ngai Tahu and Lecturer in History, University of Canterbury, 2005.

Southerly

Laura Keddell

Fiction

It was starting to rain and through his kitchen window Everett could see his neighbour's washing on the line, flapping in the biting southerly. He stood frozen with indecision. He didn't even know that woman; would she think he was a creep if he just popped over and brought her washing in for her? It was exactly the kind of neighbourly thing his Mum would've done. He had a flash of the exhausted face he'd glimpsed through the windscreen this morning as his neighbour had exited so rapidly. He remembered the delight in his Mum's tired voice, returning from the shops, small children buttoned up against the grim rain, to find a large basket of neatly folded washing under their porch. She had said it felt like angels had visited from heaven. That decided him. It'd been a long, long time since he'd done anything that could be called angelic.

He'd found a book last week at his op-shop over the road, Dogwatch, called *Random Acts of Kindness*, in the 20c bin. Didn't usually go in for self-help books, but this was more socialist than navel gazing. Time for action, not thinking, the book had said. Right, then. He put on his cut-down gummies and went out his driveway and up the parallel one into his neighbour's yard.

The staffy came barrelling through the pet door as he heard Everett walking up the drive and met him, growling softly at the side gate off the driveway.

'Hey, boy, Cuba, it's only me, okay?' Everett had been talking to this dog through the fence since he'd moved in six months ago. When he was out at his clothesline or compost or vege patch, the caramel snout had often pushed through plank gaps to sniff gidday. He'd seemed friendly enough, so Everett had decided to risk it.

The basket was right there, but he wondered what she did with her pegs? Ah – that's right; she keeps them on her line. He'd noticed them sitting like miniature birds in one of his stoner sessions with Fasele. They'd laughed so hard they'd nearly fallen off the porch.

Flowery velvet trousers, patchwork skirts, big black knit tops. He tried to remember how to fold these clothes, but they were too far out of his usual repertoire of jeans and tee-shirts. He felt fumbly in the increasing gale. He tried to take the knickers off the line without looking at them. Black, cotton, medium, were all he allowed himself to notice.

Stockings and socks; he even found pairs and folded them together.

The dog was watching him, looking confused, at the bottom of the steps.

At least they were all good and dry. She wouldn't have to fight with the clothes airer she sometimes used on her porch with so much swearing and cursing that he could hear, if his kitchen window was open.

He'd wanted to offer to help her in the past, but had felt too shy. His mum had had an airer like that, and it had been his job to set it up, lay out the clothes, and then fold them and put it down the next day. He had loved how the lemony waft of clean clothes added to the other smells of home. Odd job for a boy back then, but it hadn't worried his mum.

When the basket was nearly full, he started stressing about where to put it. The porch door was shut and likely locked. Bugger, he wished he'd thought of that. He carried the basket up to the house and sure enough, it was. The staffy wasn't too hot about him being on the porch, either. Double bugger. He could feel the confusion creeping in. This was the sort of crisis he encountered daily; problem solving sent him into high anxiety. His psychologist had been giving him exercises for it, but panic was close to the surface much of the time.

There was no point leaving the clean folded washing out in the rain from which he had saved it; maybe he could leave it in her garage. But she'd never find it. A note. That's what he'd do. Great; the slowing-down-and-waiting-for-options-to-come strategy was working. He tried the garage door, balancing the basket on his hip, as the first near-horizontal drops hit the side of his head. It was locked.

BUGGER IT. The voice inside his head was screaming. He wished he'd never thought about bringing his damn neighbour's damn washing in. He had just started down her driveway, having resigned himself to taking the bloody washing to his own porch and coming back with a note, when her Corolla pulled into the driveway.

His worst nightmare.

The rain was getting going now. He wasn't wearing his hat and he was scared of this wild woman. He thrust the basket into her arms, muttered something about wanting to help, and ran to the haven of his kitchen. He could hear her calling to his guilty back. He slammed his door and sank down against it to the floor, moaning aloud at his stupidity. He realised she could see him from her driveway, through the far kitchen windows, and he leapt up and closed the dusty, rusty venetians. And sat down on the floor by the cupboards because he needed privacy to keep moaning.

The storm was building on both sides of his windows. The light around the edges of his vision was flickering to blue, then purple, then black. Floating twinklers were speeding past him, like in a galaxy far away, whenever he closed his eyes.

'We have gone where no man has gone before,' he heard being intoned inside his head. Had he said that aloud? Then that woman was at the door, banging on it.

'I know you're in there.' Bang, bang, bang. 'What were you doing at my place, with my washing?' Bang, bang, bang.

Thank God he'd replaced the glass panels for wood last year when Fasele's juggling had broken them, otherwise she'd have been able to see him rocking on the floor. The last thing he heard was her screeching.

'If I catch you messing with my washing again, I'll call ...' Then mercifully whooshing blackness.

Note: Extract from *Easterly*, a novel in progress

On the Edge

Robynanne Milford

ontheedge
sungrass snaps
a timeball

falls

vermilion rain fall
like rogue frogs in a desert
she's seen frogs cycle
from Whitehead Wash
outstepping   to the palace
between Peacocks Gallop
and Rockinghorse Road.
she knows 'it's a life cycle'
stepping out
she knows life
is

a crystal prism
– is all –
she knows
knows
a crystal staircase
forms
'bridge over troubled waters'
she has sung it on the 'stairway to'
childbirth
when the heavens opened
with waterfalls
she could swim

who needs wheels
when it's all a cycle
knows her life cycle from a bicycle
knows it's rapacious to ride up
crystal
steps

knowing that to fly
'feathers unfettered'   is

peace profound

Notes: Barry Cleavin:'It's All a Life Cycle'
Led Zepplin:'Stairway to Heaven'
Simon and Garfunkel:'Bridge Over Troubled Waters'
Karen Zelas, Galina Kim, Sue Spigel: feathers unfettered (exhibition)

Ma and Con

Lesley Evans

A memoir

I'd like you to meet Ma and Con Cunningham, our next door neighbours in Bristol Street in the Christchurch suburb of St Albans. In the 1950s, it was a fairly ordinary part of town, but nowadays it has become part of Merivale, a much more desirable address.

The Cunninghams lived quietly in a neatly painted villa, with its rarely used concrete path curving through the flower garden at the front and another path leading round the side of the house to the back door. Con had to give up his job at *The Press* after his hand was cut off by the guillotine, so he spent his days working in his double-dug vegetable garden and painting the white weatherboard house.

My sister and I were too young to be interested in the origins of our neighbours but we were fascinated with the way they talked. We'd run up to the back door and see Con standing there, chuckling at us. He'd call out, 'What ho, Leb! What ho, Pen,' and we knew we were welcome. His thatch of thick wavy hair and his strongly built frame made him look twice as tall as Ma, and I wondered if he had to pick her up to kiss her.

Ma never took off her full-length pinny or changed out of her slippers. It was strange to me, because my mother didn't believe in slippers, and she'd say, 'I wouldn't be seen dead in an apron like that!' We loved to watch Ma wringing out her long dishcloth, a soft white cotton mesh, the kind that was used to wrap the stiff sides of lamb exported from the Belfast freezing works. She'd fill the sink with hot water, rattling the soap shaker till bubbles crawled high up the sides of the tub. Her arms wet up to the elbow, Ma plunged in the dishcloth, swished and swirled it round and round, and lifted it above the foam for a triumphant celebration of the wash. It was like Dad standing at the altar raising the communion bread and wine above his head to show God how good it was. With a twist and flick, Ma would wind the cloth into a double helix, so the final act of wringing out the water could be done with ease. She really loved that dishcloth, you could see that. Not like our mother, who disdained housework. When she squeezed out a cloth her face soured, as if to say, 'I hope to heaven nobody can see me doing this!'

On Sunday mornings, when our parents and older sisters went to 8 o'clock Communion at St Mary's Merivale, Penny and I would run over next door for breakfast. Mother didn't approve and I imagine she was embarrassed about the situation, but we got far too hungry to wait till they came home to make the porridge and brown toast. Ma and Con ate all their meals an hour earlier than we did, so there was always something for us. Ma's pikelets were fantastic. She warmed up the butter in the pan, and made them one at a time so each one was a perfect thick circle. In our house there'd be five or six done at once, and they'd come out all shapes and sizes. 'Come on, Leb, have a piece,' Ma would say, offering a slice of sponge, a sugar-topped rock cake, or a scone spread with raspberry jam.

I remember looking around for books in their house, but there were none. 'Why don't you read anything, Con?' I asked with innocent bluntness.

He chuckled. 'Well, Leb, it's a long story. Once upon a time I did go to school, but it was a night school. We had to leave the windows open to let in the fresh air, and the wind blew out the candle, so I couldn't see the book. That's why I can't read like you and all your clever sisters.' I never knew whether to believe him, because he could quote the homespun philosophy on the posters that hung in his immaculate garden shed, as if he could read every word.

Our favourite time of the day was after their 5 o'clock 'tea', when Con relaxed in his high-backed chair beside the glowing coke fire. We never saw anyone sitting so still. He gazed into the flickering red shapes, moving only occasionally to rattle the black iron poker between the bars of the grate to let more air in to feed the flames. We climbed onto the arms of the chair and touched his tightly crimped hair, combing and curling it as we did at home when we played hairdressers. While Con listened to 'Dad and Dave' on the old brown radio, he was totally at our mercy. We made the game last as long as we could, until our mother called out over the fence that it was time to come home.

Patient and kind, Con had something that was in very short supply at our place: he had all the time in the world. With their only child already married, Ma and Con gave us adult attention, not so available in our big family. No wonder Pen and I have always treasured the memory of Ma and Con Cunningham and their gentle pace of life.

I Saw Sam Hunt Today

Elizabeth Robertson

I saw Sam Hunt in the
fish shop today. I was
too much in awe for any
thing to say. He leaned
long-limbed across the
counter and sang in his
lightly pedantic way for
200 grams of flounder.
It may have been all he
could pay, with the only
spare cash he had on him
that cool and friendless
Canterbury day.

It looked like he was
living in his big old car
and driving through a town
where gardens are the star
held in high regard, while
great poets go hungry.
I thought, as I walked away,
I should have helped out that
day. He has opened his soul
to us without a fuss, daring
to share his tousled dreams
in a flawless flow of words
and themes that will live, long,
after all our gardens have
withered and gone.

First published in the *BayLit* magazine, Golden Bay, 2008

Orana Octet
~ songs before a wedding ~

Jenny Powell

I
The first kiss recalled
in the Outback,
my lips on the back
of your hand

an event foretold

and Madonna kisses
the head of her infant
giraffe, a moment
remembered, recorded.

II
Cheetahs chilling out
in the beginning of day
on the edge
of a wire world.
Their markings
a map of the freckles
across your back.

III
She is content
retreating into her shell.
He is frantic
butting his head
against her, over
her, behind her.
She runs,
he follows,
aggressive ardour
climbing her back,
he bares his teeth
in a tight grimace.

Sometimes I will need
to hide in my shell.

IV
Feeding time
for the pig.
A herd of humans
dropping grapes and bits
of bananas into the gaping
mouth, head swivelling
like a sideshow clown.

When my mouth opens
in silence, the old fears

will have left me weak
and hungry.

Feed me a feast
of sweet banana pieces
and fat grapes
almost ready to burst
out of their skins.

V
Miss Jenny of the World,
graceful
tasteful
natural elegance
without embellishment,
distinctive style
with a runway smile,
hair infused
with a flood of light
fake tan refused
for soft skin delight.
Stunningly chic,
perfect physique,
femme fatale,
amorous animale.

VI
White rhinoceros
dancing downhill
to the hay.
Unhurried
despite hunger,
graceful
despite desire,
as dainty as a geisha
dancing in our Spring.

VII
You have discovered
my lost time
and now I am your pest,
pinching your beached-as belly,
pulling the hairs on your legs,
biting your ear to see
if you're awake.

I am the spider monkey
who mimics me
mimicking him,
poking out our tongues,
opening our mouths the widest,
cocking our heads to one side.

VIII
My eyes slow focus
to the shade
the smeary window
and the cavern
of a giant nostril.

My heart bungies to my feet
my hands hold on to the noise
from my mouth, I wait
for his claws to scar my skin
through the window.

He angles himself
to meet her gaze,
lady lion
lying on a rock,
their eyes locking
in a lightning line,
exploding every theory
of time and motion
in raw emotion.

Coca-Cola Jesus and Mitsubishi Mary
Christmas in the Park, Christchurch 2003

Apirana Taylor

we sit in the night and sing
'Glory to the newborn king'

beneath a plastic star
before the tinsel tree

a new car is sacrificed on the altar
who will win the keys to heaven?

wreathed with television angels
the prophets preach

'Silent night, holy night
Kolynos keeps your teeth white'

Jesus teaches, 'Things go better with Coke'

Mary rides a brand-new Mitsubishi
whose motor runs on virgin oil

MERRY XMAS FROM COCA-COLA

Apirana Taylor: *Te Ata Kura* (Canterbury University Press, 2004)

127

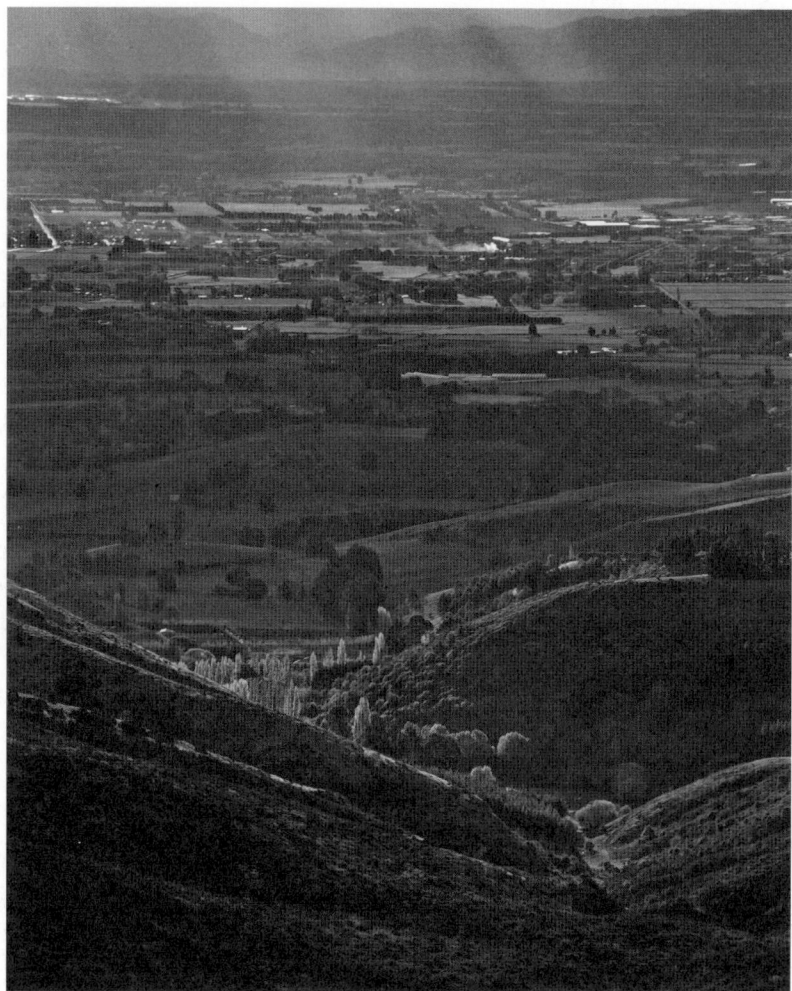

Plains

… we find certainty, knowing the land
patterned with light and careless ease.

– Tom Weston, 'Fragments'

Canterbury

Stephanie Grieve

You got pummelled all right,
beyond recognition.
Ice, apparently
desperate for a glimpse of the sea.

Nature's thug, it ran roughshod
refused compromise.
No-one was here then
to temper the violence.

There were no ground rules,
just that unholy racket as, flat
on your face, you ate dust
and blood ran braided for the coast.

Later, of course, it retreated
they always do, the great conquerors.
Its age was up, its destiny defeat
when the heat came on.

But it was too late for you
left plain indefinitely,
a doormat
on the way to the main event.

By the time they made it to the top,
any old swamp
would have looked worth settling,
they never saw a weakling.

But some still tell of nights unsettled
by the rattle tattle nor'wester
of waking with the grudge of ages:
a sting in the corner of one eye.

Nor'west Season

Helen Lowe

Waiting . . .
      the nor'west arch a pale slash
      along cloud-filled sky, promises heat –
            big bluster coming
      beating in across the plains   lifting
      roofs   tossing down
      trees   a dog howls
            into the sun's glazed eye
      falls back into shadow
            beneath a car body
      propped on a rusted jack   waits
      for the lull . . .

Remembering Taitapu

Sara Newman

A memoir

At ninety-seven years of age, Forrest Wood has a very long memory, which he loves to share. Born in Halswell, he left school at the age of twelve, in 1923, to help milk cows on the farm his father bought at Taitapu.

There is something special about 'Tai Tap', as the locals call it. I felt it as I drove down Old Taitapu Road. It was not only the still, sunny, November day, the luminous green of the mid-spring trees lining the roads, or even the friendly, generous people. In the first half of the last century Taitapu had a generous benefactor who left a legacy of community assets. Sir Heaton Rhodes blessed the community with his riches.

Taitapu is a small township curled round the Halswell River between the Port Hills and the road to Akaroa, about twenty minutes' drive from Christchurch. The English translation of Taitapu is, according to one authority, 'sacred or special waters', to another 'boundary', perhaps because the land of the Ngati Korehu hapu bounded the Taitapu (now Halswell) River.

The earliest settlers in Taitapu came from Hanover in Germany to pit-saw timber in the saw mill started by one of their countrymen, John Girkin. Their presence is remembered in names, such as John Heinzmann, whose portrait is part of a composite photograph hanging in the Taitapu Hotel, and in Osterholts Road.

In 1895 for his new wife Jessie, Heaton Rhodes, later Sir Heaton Rhodes, built Otahuna (Place of the Sandbank), his home at the foot of the Port Hills overlooking Taitapu. His name is preserved today in landmarks, such as Rhodes Park Domain and Rhodes Road, while his family is remembered in Hepworth Place, named after Epworth in Lincolnshire where Heaton Rhodes' father had been born.

By 1900 the town was well established and needed a community hall. Heaton Rhodes had previously offered one hundred pounds towards its costs, but, after fifteen years, successive committees had failed to get the project started. On 24 May 1904 a public meeting was convened and on the first page of the large, leather-bound minute book, it is recorded that the chairman 'explained that he was in receipt of a definite offer of two hundred pounds and a site towards the providing of a public hall for the Tai Tapu District.' The site chosen was known as 'Breeze's', where Jack Breeze had owned a wheelwright's shop, near the blacksmith's and the butcher's shambles, which included slaughter-house and shop. Mr Rhodes approved the site and this time the committee acted quickly, so quickly that three years later the minutes record that 'no body of men could have handled so much money in a more satisfactory manner.'

Mr Edward England of England Bros, architect, was engaged to draw up plans and Mr Robert Forbes, storekeeper, carpenter and postmaster, to build the hall for a contracted price of six hundred and forty-three pounds … They ordered their new hall to be painted turkey red with body-cream facings and dark green steps.

Three boxes of macrocarpa seedlings were ordered and planted. These grew into a fine shelter belt for the hall and later provided shelter of a different kind. Mr Wood told me that in earlier days it was illegal to consume alcohol anywhere near a hall while a dance was in progress, and a Christchurch police 'flying squad' sometimes raided the place. 'When the fence was cut years later full bottles of liquor were found among the branches. Of course no one claimed the bottles,' Mr Wood told me.

When I arrived at Mr Wood's house the appetising aroma of freshly cooked bacon filled the kitchen. His house backs onto the sultry, narrow, dark-green Halswell River. As we leaned against the bench looking out the window a rabbit surprised us both. 'They've a warren on that side of me,' he said, 'but they seem to like the grass on the other side.' Supported by his walking frame, he led me into his living room. 'I'd be good as gold if I had new legs,' he said.

Mr Wood met his wife, Joan Millar, at the hall when she was the cook at Otahuna and Jonesy, Sir Heaton Rhodes' chauffeur, drove Joan and the housekeeper, Miss Vee Vee Hynes, to the dances. 'I offered to take them home in my car after the dance,' he said and that was the beginning of his romance and long happy marriage. Jonesy, or Jockey Jones as he was also called, had been Rhodes' polo groom, batman, coachman and, when Rhodes' first attempt at driving his new 1907 Rover ended in a ditch, his chauffeur.

'Winter was the ball season; you see it was when farmers had time.' Each sports club held an annual ball. He showed me charming invitations, 'requesting the pleasure of _____', which were sent out from The Bachelors of Tai Tapu, The Ladies of Tai Tapu, the Employees of Otahuna etc, and on each of these early invitations was written 'Grand March 8pm'. By 1950 the Grand March was no longer on the programme.

The balls were grand occasions. The names of those attending were sent to the Christchurch papers for publication in the social pages. 'I remember men in dress suits and women in beautiful gowns,' said Mr Wood. An air of excitement filled the room as the band struck up. 'The balls always started with the Grand March in which all the couples paraded round the hall, then formed sets of eight for the most popular dance, the Valetta. Occasionally there was a 'ladies engage' dance, giving the girls a chance to dance with the bashful boys. The yard would be full of horses and gigs and bicycles … We had sit-down suppers, you know, with cream and fruit salad. The men's conveniences were down the back and the women had a two-seater, outside, near the women's cloakroom.' It sounded quite a sociable arrangement for the women, who could share the wooden bench, with two holes above the cans.

In this heyday of social activity one entertainer stands out. 'Dinah Lee; do you remember Dinah Lee? She sang here, you know, as part of the Halswell Women's Institute Concert Party.' The name was familiar; I did remember Dinah Lee and checked up on her career. She was the first Kiwi artist to top the Australian charts and she sang to an audience in the Taitapu Hall. Forrest Wood had never forgotten her and the sound that would later be described as 'bright, poppy and gutsy'.

Mr Wood told me there were once large portraits of Sir Heaton and Lady Rhodes above the doorway and portraits of committee members in four-inch oak frames around the walls. These have gone. In the foyer, now, hang eight committee members' portraits which came from Otahuna and a photograph of the old hall. The names of the men from Taitapu who served in the two world wars and those who died, fourteen in World War I and eight in World War II, are recorded on two handsome, wooden Rolls of Honour.

The hall was also used for lectures, concerts, bazaars and flower-shows – Otahuna was renowned for its daffodils. They were a passion of both Heaton Rhodes and his head gardener. Indeed the sale of flowers and imported bulbs, together with prize money and proceeds from the flower shows, raised more than one thousand pounds; enough money to build a library.

At the opening of the handsome little stone building in 1932, Governor General Lord Bledisloe referred to the flower shows at the official opening: 'I have never before heard of the flowers of the field being converted into the flowers of literature,' he said. He also said of Sir Heaton Rhodes, 'Apparently he spends his leisure thinking out means whereby he can do good to his fellow men – the people among whom he lives.' That same spirit is still apparent in the community today and in the generous manner with which Mr Forrest Wood shared his memories.

References:

Ogilvie, Gordon, *The Port Hills of Christchurch* (Reed, 1978)

Rice, Geoffrey W., *Heaton Rhodes of Otahuna* (Canterbury University Press, 2001)

Wood, Forrest, *Tai Tapu, The Way It Was* (unpublished)

Just a Drop of Water

Mary Keaveny Costello

What did you see, clear water, as you ran
Over the coloured pebbles
Through Waimakariri stream?
That all the pretty stones could boast
Was only of your making?
In a drying sun
All are grey as one.
What did you feel, soft vapour, as you rose
Into the warmth the sun had drawn you to?
Just that it was your duty to return
With the cool clammy draught of evening air –
Wake on an early morning flower,
To find yourself cast there?
Where are you now, dewdrop among the green?
Soft on a Stewarts Gully plot,
Or farther flown,
Hearing the grind of trucks
On the highway,
Touching and clinging fast to petal face:
Until again the sun will draw you up and up,
And pelt you back as heated Summer rain?
Can you choose your favoured path?
Northwards to seek the Tropic arms?
Or must the natural ever-turning wind
Lose you for aeons in Antarctic ice
Among a million million of your kind?

From a manuscript entitled: *August In The Placid City*, placed in the New Zealand Room of the Christchurch City Library in the 1970s.

Thrillseeker's Canyon

Ellie Cradwick

Depth
Looking down
Height
So far to fall
Down
One foot
Shaking
Finds the edge
Nudging empty space
Nothingness
I breathe sharp air
Deep breath
Fill my lungs
And then
I let
Myself
Fall …

I stop
Nose grazing the surface

Up
Up
Arms spread wide as wings
Swinging
World upside-down

I see the jet boat leave
And they pull me on board
Untie the cord
Back
To live again
With adrenalin pumping …

I did it.

Note: Ellie is aged 14

If Trees Could Speak

kimbala

Creative nonfiction

> *Gates act as barriers. They keep things in. They suggest by their closure that things might be kept out.*

My father's old farm gates frame a window on the outside world. On his six-acre property the view is largely obscured by dense hedges and trees. Weathering silently on solid posts buried deep in the earth his gates mark the entrance to an old driveway. Over their long timber slats and double-x bracing you can see clear to the Southern Alps. It is the best of views.

The gates are seldom opened any more, not since the new driveway, cattle stopped and un-gated, was installed. The old driveway was made straight and wide enough for tractors, combine harvesters and sheep trucks. Gated, we presume, to keep stock from wandering.

The new driveway is curved, narrow, shingled and dusty – prone to pot-holing in winter. It runs closer to the houses so that vehicles, motorbikes and boats can be parked for a more convenient and speedy egress.

> *A nor'west breeze blows the scent of potato flowers across the road. Gentle white clouds of perfume.*

Nine people live in the two houses to which the new driveway leads. Five in the old sprawling weatherboard farm-house. Four in the new plaster-coated aluminium-windowed polystyrene house. The retirement home of my parents. Post-divorce, post-belated OE, I am a recent addition. My boy followed me home. There are suddenly vehicles everywhere.

> *Wheat shifts silver under a full circle of moon. Rustles; wrestles with an easterly wind.*

My father lives for this place. Tends the trees as if they were old friends, raises chooks and raspberry canes. Mows and trims and pulls and sprays. Keeps order. The land rewards him. The garden hums with a peace and serenity not often found in the outside world.

The outer world returns on the faces of those who must leave, for work and for school, beyond the dense hedges of pine. It returns in their stance, their walk and their words – and in the chiming clatter of the cattle-stop rails.

At times the outside world intrudes unbidden – an unknown man is discovered looking for trout in the stream, a car enters a paddock to carve up the earth at speed, a secretive dumper pitches plastic and paper over a fence. The row of letter-boxes, of which ours is the first, is toppled in the night.

An eyebrow of rain-cloud hangs over the mountains.
Hovers there – impassive, grey-green.

One morning I watched my father shuffle out towards the gates. He doesn't walk really any more. Can't lift his legs the way he once did. But he shuffled in his dignified manner to discover the damage, to pick up the pieces and to wonder at how such things happen.

One half of the gates lay on the ground, smashed off its hinges, the cross bars in splinters and shards. The remaining half clung twisted and useless to the hinges that had marked their time, holding that gate in its place, fifty years or more. The bolts were rusting through. You could see that clearly now. There had been no outward sign of this aging before. Only the timbers, bleached down to that grey-green algae colour gates and fences go.

Hawk wheels and flaps and dips over the wheat field.
A cloud of sparrows disperse into a tree.

He laid the pieces of gate out on the parking space beside the garage. Hauled them up from the front of the property by hand-drawn trailer. Heavy pieces. Lifting the larger piece off the hinges can't have been easy for him.

We looked at the remains like two surgeons looking over a broken body.

'Well, it's disappointing,' he said, 'but I guess it's a sign of the times. People don't own up to things like they used to.'

I nodded agreement, thinking about how and why things change.

Water canons chuff silver against the summer blue.
Sucking the aquifers dry.

Come Saturday morning, the reparation of the gates had been given status within the wider family. Three generations of men stretched over its long frames with drills, hammers, nuts and bolts. Their movement – the whacking of nails, the pressure on the drill, the lifting and the turning – surrounded by displaced timbers scattered like iron filings around a magnet.

The youngest among them, dispatched unexpectedly to a hardware store for parts to replace the worn out and the broken. I watched him walk towards his uncle's vehicle, elated to be driving again after his DIC. Promoted back into a position of trust. A swing to his step. A step forward, and a step back.

A summer haze ripples the buildings, bushes and hills.
Corrugates and distorts the landscape.

We women talked, as women do on a Saturday morning, lulled by the ease of the weekend. Standing around in the winter sun watching the workers, theories abounded.

'This was no accident, ya know. This was wilful. Same young hoons that pulled out our letter boxes. More of their – *what is it?* – mindless vandalism. Makes my blood boil to see Dad having to repair heavy gates like these. If I could get my hands on that lot, I'd fill their pockets with some loose change.'

'Could have been the wind, you know. Blew up pretty smart the other morning. Round five it came through with a wallop. You wouldn't have heard a thing over the roaring in the trees.'

'Gate might have been left unlatched. Wind might have slammed it back on itself. It's a funny thing, wind.'

'Wasn't *wind*. There's car tracks down there in the dust beside the hedge. None of us would've pulled in like that. Reckon someone's driven in hard and whacked the gate.'

'Would've left a hell-u-va dent in a car. There's no paint on the timbers and no broken glass.'

'Must've been something large then. One of those four-wheel-drive jobs with bull bars or a truck.'

'Yeah? But it was a Wednesday night – a *week* night.'

We walked down through the avenue of trees towards the gate posts. There *were* tracks in the dirt by the hedge. Wide tyres. Not car tracks. Faint markings where a vehicle had pulled in and turned. Wind didn't make those.

> *A silver tower of pylon reaches for the sky.*
> *Its head is in the clouds.*

Stray questions festered and spread within the family during the rest of that week. It was strangely unnerving – the knowledge of intrusion. Questions that brought the young among us under suspicion, revealed our defensiveness and our readiness to defend.

'Who brought Sam home that night?'

'His girlfriend's mother!'

'Ohhh. Don't suppose she'd know anything about it, then?'

'How come you didn't hear anything from your place?'

'We never do. Sleeping on the other side of the house.'

'Johnny wouldn't know anything?'

'Why would he?'

Curious how unexplained events unnerve us. A whiff of suspicion. A vague sense of culpability. In an ideal world somebody would own up.

> *A white butterfly skips over the grass.*
> *Rests on a pinecone.*

I find myself drawn to the towering trees. Standing sentinel along the grassed-over entrance from that other time, they watch. Having once lined a gracious and ample driveway to a much grander house – the original farm-house that burned down years ago – they watch over everything, still. If only they could speak.

Oak and sycamore, eucalyptus and elm. Tall. Their roots run deep in the streambed to their right and suck the life from the grass-sown soil to their left. These are trees with integrity. Standing their ground even in the fiercest of winds that scream in from the south and smash in from the north-west. Their stories would be tall stories. Histories of people, farm-workers, horses, machines. The grunt and the gruff – the metal of the working farm.

Tall grey boughs, sweep the reaches of sky.
The eucalyptus trees
creak and sough in the wind.

Like old bones with new clothing, the gates are back now, in their place at the front. Three generations lifted them back into place, dropped the latch to hold them secure and stepped back to admire the work.

'Mutton dressed as lamb,' my mother says. 'They're a bit of a patch-work eye-sore. We'll have to paint them – tidy them up a bit.'

My father demurs. 'They're okay like this.'

I look to my father, the stoop in his body and the frailness of bone. With his hand gripping the top rail there is no hint of the shaking that dogs him. Instead – a kinship with his gates – their respective strengths tested through adversity. His eyes look out over the best view.

There is something stately and proud about the way those gates hang on. Old, but patched and still vital. My father is patched also. His patches come in boxes of fifty. My mother is constantly looking for fresh places to shave him for the next application. His Parkinson's medication is disseminated this way – quietly diffusing through skin.

Sun sets in the pale south-west.
The mauve hush of evening creeps across the sky.

141

The Farm

Janet Wainscott

A memoir

I remember open space and winds racing across the plains and lazy summer clouds forming pictures in the sky. The blue-domed sky was immense and we were always reading it, watching the change from nor'west arch to southerly bank and waiting for the drought to break or the rain to stop. I remember the sheep and the ripening wheat, the dogs and the dust, the frost and the sun. I thought it would never change.

Our farm was near the edge of a river of melted snow, braiding its way through islands of stones. The land was flat, fertile and endless. I'd only seen the farm once in the thirty years since my parents sold it, and then one day in early summer my sister and I decided to drive past where we had once lived.

'It *feels* the same,' said Ali, as we got out of the car and stood on the grass between the gorse hedge and the gravel road. During droughts we had spent summer afternoons lying in that grass minding a mob of sheep, one of us at each end, reading or daydreaming, as the sheep foraged along the roadside to eke out the feed.

It *sounded* the same. The birds from the hedges and the neighbouring farms were in full voice but there was no other sound. I thought of a winter morning long ago when I had walked along the gravel road on the way to the school bus, crunching the ice in the puddles. That morning the row of trees across the road was black in silhouette with the sun rising behind. I had turned and looked at the mountains, soft blue, snow-laden and draped in pink shadows. In the trees a thrush puffed out his breast and broke the silence, singing as if he would live forever.

Nothing *looked* the same. For a start, the shelter belts of trees we'd planted had been ripped out. 'Remember watering those shelter belts?' Ali said. How could I not? We had filled a forty-gallon drum, bucket by bucket, from the water race and driven it on a trailer to the trees, then emptied it, bucket by bucket. Our hands blistered and shoulders ached and the sun burnt our skin.

Now the trees, the stitching that held together the pieces of the plains, were gone, together with the fences, all the internal fences, not just from our farm. With amalgamations, our old farm had become part of a much larger block, close to a thousand acres, a few huge paddocks of struggling wheat.

The land used to be capable of growing a decent crop of wheat, in a proper crop rotation, so long as there wasn't too bad a drought. Dad took a photo once of a bumper crop with Grandad, me, my brother and my sister – oldest to youngest, tallest to shortest – lined up in the paddock. The wheat was almost ready to harvest. It was up to Grandad's waist, my chest, my brother's shoulder and Ali's chin. The dog was with us, but he was just a blur in the photo. As he ran through the wheat he had to jump every few yards, like a swimmer taking breath, to get his bearings.

One of the owners in recent years had sunk a well; in our day the well-diggers couldn't get deep enough to strike water. Now the owner towed his irrigation rig across the land, watering on a scale we could never have imagined and taking crop after crop off the land. I looked towards the hills and saw no animals.

Ali summed up the unfamiliar landscape: 'There's just a big hole where we grew up.'

We were raised in the heyday of the family farm, but ours was the generation that left. We had to, especially the girls, for work, for education. We wanted to travel, and we travelled as far as we could. Some of us came back, but not to the farms, just to the cities or towns an hour or two's drive, or a toll call away.

The house was just visible. The original was cramped and lacked charm and comfort, so no sentimentality there. It was now workers' accommodation and that showed how much things had changed; hardly anyone employed workers when we were kids. As for the house on the farm next door, you'd have needed an archaeologist to find any trace of it.

We saw the overgrown garden and could just make out the curve of the driveway. When we looked carefully we could see many of the trees that Dad had planted over forty years ago – oaks, clumps of silver birches, rhododendrons now collapsed and sprawling over the remains of the lawn; kowhai along the water race. Dad used to say that by the time Ali and I were married it would be a splendid setting for a wedding marquee. It would have been, but we didn't oblige. Neither of us saw ourselves as suitable material for a farmer's wife. Nor did the local farmers' sons.

We drove away in our own cloud of dust to the end of the gravel road and then onto the tar seal and past farms that still looked like the one we grew up on. It was an odd little pocket of farms that the dairy cows hadn't reached yet.

Our next stop was the former two-teacher school, long-closed now. There we learnt the 3 R's and did as we were told, long before teachers had heard of self-esteem.

Next door to the school, through a gap in the macrocarpas, was the community hall, a gathering place and venue for school break-ups, farewells, monthly church services, flower shows, kitchen teas, card evenings, indoor bowls, Sunday school concerts.

The hall was one of the last bastions of the ladies-a-plate social functions. Farmers' wives in the 1960s baked prodigious quantities of scones, pikelets, cakes, biscuits and slices to feed their physically active families. Bear in mind that baking was one of the few competitive outlets available to these women, and you might glean some idea of how sumptuous these afternoon teas and suppers were, and how exciting for a child. We were drilled in the appropriate etiquette: take one thing at a time, start with something plain or savoury before reaching for the cream cakes.

As we pulled up we saw a hawk sitting on the side of the road, staring at us. Its feathers gathered all the colours of the land, the dun dust of drought, the sheen of a freshly ploughed furrow, the fleck of wheat gold. We soon saw that the bird was close to death and on the ground because its wing was broken and flapping helplessly. We tried not to think about it as we drove back to town, the reproach in the hawk's hard eyes.

I doubt that I will go that way again.

Evening in the Canterbury Plains

Jan Hutchison

Night's here.
We look out to paddocks
where earth and wheat lie together
God tunes his deaf ear all ways
into nothingness ...
You did not wait to be *gathered like grain*.
You lived inside the word *is* as that word
lives in a sentence.

If I were a she-hare guarding a leap of leverets
I'd listen for the twitch of grasses.
My form would shadow every stem.
Tonight, the breath of cows and the thickset
pony will warm us.

Riding Out

Ruth Arnison

Over at the stables we assemble apple boxes
into Quarter Horses, making do with sack
saddles, twine stirrups

Whistling our dogs to 'come by' we ride out
side by side accompanied by cantering
commentary

Taking turns we open gates, leaning forward
on the ascent, sparingly using flax whips

Today exercising two Black Beauties, tomorrow
we'll be Phar Lap's jockeys discussing
our chances

at the Riverton Races. Wading through the waves
Smithfield's stink permeates the air,

reminding us of tonight's roast. Turning to call
the dogs we're suddenly conscious
of being observed

by the neighbours. Dismounting, we knock over
our apple box dreams, abandoning them
to the back lawn

In Which She Is Because of a Horse

Claire Hero

Out of the stall, a foaling, what seems a beginning. A stirring
in her womb that is an engine.

Something tethered on small ropes.

She thinks she cannot be broken now. Be bridled. Cannot be
saddled.

The bag between her legs: plastic or membrane?

A chafe, & a fouling. A bit.

Horses are stabled inside her, or she is stabled inside a horse.
Horse upon horse upon horse.

Her breasts are small foals & she sells them. She rides them hard.
She loves a cracked whip. A salt lick.

A faint whiff of piss.

The thing she is waving, it is not white. It is not goodbye.

It is a picture of a woman, pretty pretty.
A picture of a woman young & young &
she saddles her womb & rides after.

She is one who sees through the horse to herself.
Pretty pretty.

From out of her desires fall many foals.

Claire Hero: *Sing, Mongrel* (Noemi 2009)

Brassica in Culverden

James Norcliffe

There was that time
after the heavy rains
when the road was
littered with turnips.

In the half-light they could
have been disembodied
skulls devoid of features:
Golgotha in the headlights.

We slowed right down
to a reverential crawl,
negotiating the strange
harvest in a careful slalom.

Higgledy-piggledy and
bloodless, the turnips
shone ivory white in
the slope of the rain,

as if the dark paddocks
on either side had given
up our grandparents and
their parents before them,

scattered them like turnips,
challenging us to scrunch
roughshod all over them, to
turn their memory into paste.

They came upon us too soon,
of course, and it would have
been dangerous to swerve
to avert the inevitable soft

squish as those we could
not avoid spread beneath
our tyres in an almost mute
yet quite exquisite protest.

Taumutu

Paul Bensemann

Creative nonfiction

I fly. Sweeping under waves just before they break, I glance to where the old people sit underground, looking out to sea. I know why they chose this place, back five hundred years or more, because he told me.

Above the surf I follow their gaze. Once again, close by, black backs of whales rise from the swells every few minutes or so. That was a sign for events, he said; an omen for change.

Just above the beach now, dragging my feet through pikao, the weavers' rare grass, I soar along Kaitorete Spit into Lake Ellesmere. Waihora, he called it – The Vast Water. I turn, heading for the house, and my finger-tips cut along the surface, spooking eel and flounder, his favourite foods.

Over lake-side paddocks, rabbits run for burrows. I used to shoot some, but not enough to let the grass grow long. I pass above the fence we tried to fix, he and I, and see, yet again, all the wires are slack.

Following the sand-dune, one of few points of higher ground, I peer into circular pits in the grass. He probed sometimes, with testing half-truths, wanting us to stay and learn slowly. His ancestors scooped out dunes for gardens, he said, with sparkling eyes. At least, he went on with a chuckle, that was what archaeologists decided.

Travelling upwards, into a windbelt, I weave through tips of trees along the line, once again savouring the smell of macrocarpa. The 110-year-old house is beside me, and below on the verandah I picture him, fleetingly, brown woollen hat and green-checked bush-shirt, sitting back against a house wall, both arms across the outside table, holding a teacup.

The house is empty now. I circle it. Each door and window is open and curtains drift, gently backward and forward, with the breeze. After flitting through an upstairs window, and into rooms with dozens of mattresses stacked, I feel once more an early morning happiness, bouncing down the stairway.

Heading for the marae, I cross his front block's orchard, fruit hanging, rotting; our four days' pruning work wasted. A morepork sits

149

on a gatepost, as it did when we drove off that day at noon. It stares at me, eyes showing no emotion.

Passing through a gap in an earth-wall across the road, I hover by the plain-looking hall, or meeting house, with its small sign saying, Ngati Moki. The old people built the wall, he said. They carved the land, but not a house.

Above the porch I see three of us – Elsie, her uncle and me, the population that day of Taumutu – waiting for a tourist bus from Christchurch. We learnt of generations-old kawa, rituals we should use with visitors. We spent the morning practising Elsie's karanga, my mihi, and songs we would sing with him.

Embarrassed as they arrive now, I bank away, while they surge on, enveloping us, without waiting for karanga or speeches. As I pass behind the meeting house, I hear him laughing, louder and louder, while someone photographs him, and others stare. It was funny, he said afterwards, because they thought him stupid.

Behind the building the fantail, his kaitiaki, or guardian, flitted around as we sat, just he and I, in the grass, watching small wisps of steam escape from a hangi pit. His words painted a picture hundreds of years old of islands built from carted sand and stones in a deep, wide swamp. The islands had room for the living only and, surrounded by fish and birds, were safe from attack and hunger. One sanctuary, behind the beach, was now the churchyard; the other, he said, we were on.

I head east. To my right we wandered along the creek. It did not have a Maori name, he said. It had three. The creek was a canoe route between islands. It was once the people's watercress garden and his. Now he was forced to pay drainage rates, and each month a county digger scraped out young plants. He stopped and puffed from the effort of laughing.

To my left I see us walking along the church road: he halted to catch his breath every 20 metres or so, and was serious, pointing to empty pieces of paddock, an event here, a family there. Nothing moves along the coast except two swans, rising up from below me, lazily extending their long necks horizontally, as they beat their wings in slow motion, and head away.

I listen again to pebbles rolling back with the surf – 'ssh, ssh' – and glide toward the beach, but not as far as the old people. He rests, alone, beside the church. I dive down through the earth, and embrace him.

Ashley River

Charlotte Trevella

Smell of wood-smoke
   and gorse
     rises
towards a mottled sky.

Bare trees
  stretch brittle
    fingers upwards.

And the river
  slips
    down through
a spider's web
of channels
that mingle
the mountain sand
and shingle.

Both drift towards
  a lonely sea.

Note: Charlotte was 11 years old when this poem was written.

First published in anthology of Waimakariri Poetry Competition 2004 (Waimakariri District Council, 2004)

A Dry River-bed

Jan Hutchison

Mosquito words arrive from the north

the woman walks the Hawken river-bed
and draws a hood
across her mind

through the gorse, an old plough
sizzles

thistles rise as if they were captains
who marched through dust

her breath slows
she could be a leaf of willowherb

among the boulders among the lichens
a decade passes under a lizard's eyelid

the woman regards the river-bed
now it's starred with blue borage flowers

Published in *Takahe* 67, August 2009

Down the Bluegums Road

Tracey Sullivan

Magpies gargle and yodel and caw
in the ragged, wind chewed macrocarpa
trees and in the windbreak pines before
the shadow peters out to sun glare,
and an early nor'west wind kicks up

the dust. A child squints into the sun.
Her mother trundles an old fashioned
pram over newly graded shingle
thick as waves of setting concrete. This
is the pilgrimage for mail, and milk
that's left twice weekly on the corner
in a white plastic billy with a
red plastic lid and a handle to
swing from the back of the pram.
The child scuffs and slides on the stones for
a while then walks with her hand on the
pram asking sensible questions like
who made god and where does the wind go.
The mother's head is blurred from loneliness
and lack of sleep and boredom. She tries to
form the necessary words but then
the child is darting off for treasure;
pine cones, dandelions and yarrow,
and she is left again to focus
on the distant stand of bluegums that
is rattling in the wind and breathing
eucalyptus down on dusty sheep.
In the rural delivery box where
the billy waits, milk froth settles and
the cream is rising to the top. In
the distant Southern Alps the Mt Cook
daisies bask and bloom in the sun
and silence and on the plains the wheat
grows warm and pale. The child crouching,
shades her eyes and squints into the sun.
She hesitates, then calls and runs across
the rutted ground to catch her mother.

Willowgrove

Belinda Lansley

A memoir

T hat's where your great-grandmother grew up,' Mum would say
as we drove past the old farmhouse at Ohoka, a thirty-minute
drive north of Christchurch. She would point to the top of the roof
sticking out from behind a scruffy pine tree hedge. It was only when
the trees were taken down in February 1997 and we could see the
whole house from the road that Mum and I decided to visit. We drove
up the driveway with a framed picture of the house in the 1900s and
knocked on the door of the new farmhouse, a 1970s red brick resi-
dence. The people there were renting and said that we were welcome
to look around the old house, but that we should not venture upstairs
as it was rotting.

We approached the farmhouse and were surprised at how small it
was. The grand photo of Willowgrove, as it was once called, was quite
deceiving. The weatherboards were now completely bare of their white
paint. I had seen many derelict houses such as this surrounded by shelter
belts on the harsh Canterbury plains and they all echoed something of
times gone by and a sadness that they had not been maintained. This
house was important to our family history and we had to have a taste
of what it would have been like to live there so long ago.

My three-times-great-grandparents, Karl Meng and his wife, Elise,
from Germany, had bought this property around 1873. I have not
found records on whether they built the house or whether it existed
when they purchased the property. They had seven daughters but only
three survived to maturity. One of the survivors was my great-great-
grandmother. She inherited the property and brought up her own chil-
dren there, who included my great-grandma, Dorothy Lord, who was
now 96 and living in a rest home in Christchurch. She talked about
her childhood home with a faraway look in her eyes; how she had hair
so long she could sit on it, how she rode a horse to school. She loved
living there. If she had known we were visiting, she would have wanted
to come, but to see the house in such disrepair would have broken her
heart.

We entered a door on one side of the house and saw a small sink of about 30cm by 20cm. Below the sink were a few cupboards. Next to the miniature kitchen was a walk-in pantry, probably large enough to store all the food needed on the farm. A coal range would have been used years ago, but this was no longer present. We walked into a cloak room with brass hooks behind the door. Mum tried to pull one off, thinking that it might be original and she could take it home as a memento, but it would not budge. We ventured through a door off the kitchen into the dining room with its brick fireplace. The lounge fireplace backed onto it, the two fireplaces sharing one chimney. The lounge had an exterior door which stood open at a crooked angle giving a hint of the rough pasture outside.

In the photo, Willowgrove had perennial borders, which were most probably tended by my great-great-grandfather, Edwin Lord. He loved gardening and we have photos of him leaning on a hoe as he cleared between his vegetables. There were no signs of any flowers now. The property was vacated by our family in 1918, after Edwin contracted the 1918 flu and became too weak to look after it. They sold it and moved to Papanui Road, Christchurch, but my great-grandma left a piece of herself there which she still talked about.

The whole place was rotting. A loose beam hung above our heads. There were two little bedrooms downstairs. From my great-grandma's description of the house, the front bedroom belonged to her brother, Carly. We have pictures of him, a curly blonde boy with a sweet smile, a sickly child who had to sleep downstairs near his parents until his death at seven years from diphtheria. We found his room lined with peeling wallpaper, the layers of time stripped away, back to ancient newsprint. The wind blew through and there was a hint of sadness.

The most fascinating thing was the double staircase, which split in a V-shape into separate upstairs halves of the house. The stairs were extremely steep and narrow, rather like stairs for an attic or loft. There were four rooms upstairs, according to Great-grandma, one of which was her own bedroom as a child. In the photo of the house, her bedroom had the window open. I could imagine her there, her head out, breathing in the country air, her long plait dangling. The room next door was her sister May's bedroom and the two at the back of the house were used for workmen staying overnight; of course, there was a wall separating the two girls from the other rooms to ensure privacy. I looked up the staircases but I heard the tenant's words: 'Don't go upstairs. It's rotten.' I wanted to see my great-grandma's bedroom, to see the sloping roof and the dormer window. I wanted to imagine her dolls lined up on the bed, as she had described, but I did not go up.

Mum and I walked away, out the front door, with photos and the satisfaction that we had seen a part of our history. We never told my great-grandma we had been there. She sat in the rest-home completely oblivious, dreaming of the white house with perennial borders, paddocks full of sheep and her pet pig waiting for her at the gate when she got home from school. A couple of months later she died and the next time we went past the house it had been bulldozed down.

A Fish out of Water

Barbara Strang

The Canterbury Mudfish
was unknown before 1924.

That year Mr Alfred Burrows and his son
also called Alfred, were digging a well
on their farm at Oxford,
and found in the mud

some small slim fish,
each doubled up in a chamber
shaped like a coconut.

They sent a specimen
to the Dominion Museum
and it was named in their honour
Neochanna burrowsius.

The Canterbury Mudfish
can survive out of water for sixty days,
breathing through its skin

in a state of suspended animation,
ready to swim as soon as
the waters come.

The Canterbury Mudfish is
preyed on by eel and trout

but lives where no other fish can
in small streams that dry out over summer.

Once thought to be almost extinct …

there may be thousands left
perhaps in the mud beneath your feet
waiting for rain.

Note: This poem uses phrases from various found material.

Nor'wester in the Cemetery
William Sutton's painting

Tony Beyer

if only the dead
no longer heard the wind
the bare grief
of the grassheads' course
among stones
would suffice for lamentation

struck too often
by heavenly brightness
the church roof fades
from the ridge down
a pale reverse
the negative of charring

in the upper quarter
dark tree trash flapping
where parts of the sky
have fallen out
and an angel gestures
like an auctioneer

spry and wiry
the ground's pelt
is that of a large
well camouflaged predator
or smoke that hazes away
solidity and certainty

seedheads in flecked
sandy paint
almost boil off the surface
in the laval clash
of opposing rhythms
at the still centre

its place in the canon
attested to
by pencil shavings
on the gallery floor
in front of those passages
of shadowless line

one stone in the shape
of a spatula or baby teat
crowned urns
like oil drilling bits
and a lamp flame or
door knob frozen in stone

half sunken
a quadrangular cap
like a terracotta
drainage junction
or diving helmet
to unimaginable depths

porcelain roses
congealed under a bell jar
the immobile gears
of a clock
in which time
has seeped to a stop

the ruler-straight edge
where the plain becomes hills
and the cloud river
torn off and left ragged
invite but
obstruct departure

putrid begetters
aloof in their earth stalls
backs to the hot light
compare their era
with ours with its
burnt buildings and skeletons

Tony Beyer: *Human Scale* (Sudden Valley Press, 2002); *Dream Boat: selected poems* (HeadworX, 2007)

Queen Mary Hospital Hanmer

Kerrin P. Sharpe

three o'clock she sits
on the hospital verandah
her thoughts in the thermal pools
like fern-wrapped sushi

she remembers her baby
so still he could be dreaming
and calls his name
John Graham Carr

but he is climbing
the family tree
b. 31.5.1914
d. 31.5.1914

a pine that is
really the breeze
a fish that is
really a stone

his mother
Florence Josephine Carr
that is
really himself

Long After Our Argument, Your Silence
Hanmer Springs

Helen Yong

How I like the peaked roofs and gables,
the different shades of the timber chalets:
redwood, olive green,
donkey brown and ochre.

A small boy on a bike
is weaving into the wind, his helmet
psychedelic as a 60s postcard.

The rain and the sun that came
separately and together, like
energetic young lovers,
now leave behind a dull sky.

The scapula of the mountain
sheathed in ice
abandons me to this cold valley.

Hurunui River

Juliet McLachlan

On sunny mornings when the sun is
  just rising you can see the
    Hurunui's dreams, you can see
      the sky, the sun, the clouds
        in the water, you can see the world.

Note: Juliet is eight years old.

Think Tank

Lorelei Cropp

A memoir

At its northern end, the flat carpet of the Canterbury Plains folds and creases to form rolling hills and valleys, with farms, homesteads and sheds tucked into them. Our farm, Edge Hills, in the Blythe Valley was in this area.

One morning in the 1970s, my husband, Aubrey, and I were having a cup of tea and reading the mail. Our children were away at school, and the married couple who worked for us were away on holiday. We had our farm to ourselves. We discussed what we would do together for the rest of the day – my husband hated working by himself and I always enjoyed being up on the hills at the back of the farm with a view in all directions and nobody else about for miles around. We decided to take our lunch and go to the highest point on our hill, where we had a leaking 5000-gallon water tank. We would paint the inside with a waterproof sealant.

I threw some food together and packed our gear into the Bomb, an old Model A Ford that Aubrey had converted into a do-everything vehicle. He had cut the back out, removed the back seats and fitted a timber deck floor. It was used to cart fencing gear, bales of hay or any dead sheep he found. I put the lunch under the passenger seat so the dog could not sniff it and jammed the binoculars down between the two seats. I had a tin of sealant between my feet, so it would not tip over. The dog claimed his spot on somebody's old homespun jersey in the back with the ladder and paint brushes.

We had five hundred acres of flat to drive across and then up onto the 500-acre hill block. Aubrey drove and I opened the gates; up the airstrip, past the super bin – some starlings flew out; they were having another go at nesting there after being thrown out twice. At the first gate the Angus bull was waiting, but I managed to open and shut it again before he could push his way through. Further up the flat the wild turkeys were making gobbling noises and flapping up onto a gate where they had been roosting all night, judging by the droppings underneath.

The next gate was at the start of the hill block, on a slope. The brakes were not very good, so Aubrey had to slip the clutch and gun the engine so that the Bomb did not run back on me while closing the gate. The track wound up the hill through manuka and past clay banks to the top where we drove along the spine of the hills, past tussock and cabbage trees. I liked to look from my kitchen window at these trees, silhouetted against the morning sky.

Finally we arrived at the tank and decided to eat our lunch before starting work. We sat facing the sea, each with our back to a tussock. Aubrey talked to his dog, rubbed its ears and fed it crusts, then lay down to gaze at the sky. I used the binoculars, focusing on the flat green paddocks to the south where the neighbour's cattle and stud horses grazed. Beyond them was Motunau with fishing boats waiting to get into the river mouth on the incoming tide. Across Pegasus Bay, further south again, Christchurch was a blurry haze. To the east Banks Peninsula looked as if cut out of blue cardboard and I could see the gleam from the windscreen of a car as it drove along the Summit Road. At the end of the Peninsula, a top-heavy container ship stood off the Heads waiting to enter Lyttelton Harbour. I swivelled the binoculars to the north, focusing on orange buoys marking crayfish pots, and beyond them Kaikoura.

I did not turn to the landscape behind me, but enjoyed the view in my mind's eye. I knew that in the distance high against the sky would be the Seaward and Inland Kaikouras still with a sprinkling of winter snow. Outlined in front of them the foot hills would be blue and purple. Closer still about twenty kilometres away there would probably be a wisp of smoke indicating our village. Nearer still the rolling hills with dark blotches of pine plantations. Finally our valley below, a patchwork of fenced paddocks, farm houses and shelter belts, with the road and the river snaking down to the sea. I could visualise the brown roof of our homestead just showing above the trees planted to keep out the cold sou'west wind. In our paddocks on the flat would be white sheep, black cattle and the turkeys settled down to graze.

It was time to get to work. Aubrey placed the ladder against the tank and we climbed up to squat on the top while we pulled the ladder up and then inserted it through the round hole, so we could climb down inside.

The tank had been drained, and we started painting the sealant on from the bottom up. We worked on opposite sides and as I painted and stared at three metres of concrete wall, I thought of the sea out there on the other side. I thought of my forebears sailing down the coast to Lyttelton in 1851. I wondered aloud if my grandfather could have stood on the deck of that sailing ship with his family and gazed at these hills. Would he have visualised a descendent of his in a concrete tank on this hill a hundred years later? Aubrey, practical man that he is, said, 'Of course not. Cement wasn't invented until 1870.' We continued to paint in silence.

It became obvious that we would need more sealant, and it was decided I would go on painting while Aubrey went home to get some. He climbed out of the tank and I pushed the ladder up through the hole, so that he could stand it outside and get down onto the ground. I was left in an eerie silence. No sound penetrated the tank, not even the sound of a plane I saw fly overhead against the blue sky. I did not even hear the Bomb start up and drive away.

I continued to paint until I noticed that water had started to trickle into the tank. Something must be wrong with the inlet tap. Surely Aubrey had not turned it on when he got out of the tank? No, he would not do a stupid thing like that. I continued to paint until the water covered my feet. It was then I started to panic – what if Aubrey did not come back? I had no way of getting out of the tank. The ladder was outside and the hole on top of the tank was well out of my reach. There was no other person for miles around and Aubrey was the only one who knew I was in there.

I put panic out of my mind and, to fill in time, made an effort to think about our lives and how similar they had been. We had both been born into farming families – our fathers were third generation South Island farming stock and both our mothers were from England. We had both been born in 1929, the year of the Murchison earthquake. What if there was an earthquake now? At least an earthquake would be something to write about to the children at boarding school next weekend. The water was getting deeper and I refocused my thoughts: we both went to small country schools and on to university. It was a comfort to think our children were heading in the same direction.

I made my mind a blank and continued to paint. I had no watch and no idea of the time. After a while I stopped: I felt entombed. I felt breathless – surely the paint was not giving off toxic fumes. I leaned against the wall and looked up at the circle of sky and thought at least the world was still out there. It made me feel better and I thought Aubrey would be back soon. Perhaps he was still down at the sheds leaning on the bonnet of the Bomb talking to a neighbour about the latest rainfall figures.

Painting the side facing our homestead I visualised the landscape: the Bomb crawling like a black beetle along the flat and stopping at the airstrip gate. Perhaps the Angus bull had got difficult and attacked Aubrey as he opened the gate. No, he was a West Coaster and had handled cattle all his life; he would give the bull a prod with a pitch fork – that would fix him.

Aubrey had been brought up on the wet West Coast, while I had been brought up in Canterbury, swept by the hot nor'westers. In that way our lives had been very different; the range of snow-covered Alps out there had made all the difference. Over here in Canterbury, farming had evolved more quickly and many of the pioneering skills had been lost. For instance, Aubrey always said Canterbury farmers did not know how to use a shovel properly. When he was a boy Coasters could tinker with any old engine and make it go, design or build a shed and dig a straight drain; you needed to be able to do that in the wet country. When he came to Canterbury he had to do the opposite – like installing a water scheme for the house and livestock; that is how I came to be in this water storage tank on the top of the hill in the middle of nowhere with no way to get out.

Finally I ran out of paint; I had to keep thinking.

Aubrey spoke differently. In the 1860s Australian gold miners had invaded part of the West Coast. They brought their Aussie speech and expressions with them and these lodged permanently in the speech of the old families and the farming community. Because of his manner of speaking Aubrey had often been mistaken for an Australian when we travelled overseas. Some of these Aussie/West Coast expressions still grate in my ear. 'Gidday, how ya goin'?' is one. It is appropriate in the shearing shed, but quite out of place when greeting an elderly gentleman in an English village. How I hated that expression.

More time passed, then I was startled by a sudden rush of water into the tank. It was almost up to my knees now. I comforted myself by picturing Aubrey coming up the flat past the gate on which the turkeys roosted at the foot of the hill.

The brakes. Perhaps the Bomb had run back over him as he shut the gate. No, that could not have happened; he would have parked the Bomb on an angle or left the gate open. But I could not help thinking that if Aubrey was all right he would have arrived back here long ago. Perhaps the Bomb had run off the road into a steep manuka-filled gully. I pictured it going headfirst down and the scrub springing up again, so it would be completely obscured. The ground was so hard there would not be any wheel marks to show where it had gone over. I could not bear to think of his injuries.

The water was over my knees now. What if Aubrey did not come back? Who would find him in the bottom of the gully, and who would find me floating in a tank full of water? This would be the last place the neighbours would think of looking until my body blocked the outlet and the cattle started bellowing for water. I looked up at my circle of blue sky for comfort and, as I did, a head and shoulders blocked out the light. A voice said, 'Gidday, how ya goin'?' Yes, for once I was pleased to hear it.

Just Passing Through
Under Mt Vulcan, Motunau, North Canterbury

Judith Paviell

I spend time in the shed
entranced again
at the choreography:
bend, sweep, throw –
sights, sounds, smells,
touch, camaraderie
as Radio Hauraki
blasts rock'n'roll
from a black transistor

slung from a nail
on a naked brown joist.

Sink hands and face
into still-warm fleece.
Satisfaction wells
as I wield a flat-faced broom
and the rousie says:
you've done this before.
Yes, once – yesterday.
Wistful to be part of it always,
instead of, as I am,
just visiting.

Suddenly the combs are stilled,
last sheep done for the day
and thus the deft performance.
I hover at the edge
of family and gang,
slip away across paddocks,
give the black bull a wide berth –
remain unconvinced he's a pet.

Ponder the joy of being
part of this production.
Do I weigh that as a cost of going
in a cost/benefit analysis?
or just absorb the experience,
like the symphony orchestra
nights before, whose richness
and Rachmaninoff remain
in head, heart and gut –
two orchestras, then,
double richness.

Sit with the sky's late glory –
participate for moments till it dims.
Later, on the way to bed,
stand outside and gaze
at the firmament over me,
rimmed in jagged black,
and know why firmament
is the right word.
Search for shapes among galaxies –
seek out Pleiades, newly risen.
Later still, unsleeping,
see Pleiades' moon is up –
it is like day as I say goodnight.

I think the recent freeze
has killed daisies and disarmed
the fledgling lemon tree.
That's how it goes, here –
you learn to belong
or you move on.

Driving

Maggi Belcher

Driving home I think that farming
is like writing,
at the end of the day as the writer tidies up his chapter
puts in the full-stops
the farmer shuts his gates and checks his fences.

At Darfield

Jan Hutchison

It could be like this when we start again

it's early morning
there is a copper butterfly that alights on a stone
or there are seeds of grass in the paddock

there is wheat
soon it will be the colour of the sun

listen
    the leaf stalks are rising from their bindings

and now   across the plains
             wheat glitters on a long tail of wind

and the words we surrendered in the dark
forget to look back

The ANZAC Picnic

Adrienne Frater

Fiction

Helge likes to watch them eat. Her family in Sweden rarely sits at the table, but her host family always comes together at the end of the day. As she spears peas with her fork, she watches Nadine lay her knife and fork over the cauliflower stalks, then stare at the phone. Although two years older than her host sister, Helge often feels younger. She turns towards Lance and smiles as her host father scores gravy grooves across the white china. Next to him, Cynthia dissects her last slice of beef into diminutive strips. Helge's fork hovers over her beautifully clean plate, as if undecided where to land, but her eyes remain fixed on her host mother's knife. She jumps as it clatters onto the table.

'Well,' Cynthia says, with a tight voice, 'are we going or not?'

'We're going,' says Nadine. 'Helge and I'll do the picnic, then you can get your old spreadsheet out of the way.' She nods at Helge, then looks into Cynthia's blood-shot eyes. 'OK, Mum?'

'OK, then.' Cynthia takes her glass of wine into the study and closes the door.

It had been Cynthia's idea to host an international exchange student. Lance supposed she thought it would fill some gap, compensate for some inadequacy in their family. He was quite content as they were, comfy with their 'take me as you find me' relationship, but, well used to her sudden enthusiasms, he'd agreed to the plan. From the first day, Helge had fitted right in.

'I'll get blue cheese, paté and some of those cutesy pork pies,' says Nadine, lifting down the aged picnic basket.

'And ginger beer,' Lance says with a little-boy grin. 'What about you, Helge. Any requests?'

Helge, feeling as if she was in the middle of a flight of ping-pong words, takes her time answering. 'Maybe some pumpernickel bread,' she says, pronouncing her p's with little explosions of air. When she smiles, her white teeth glow.

'I hope Mum can come,' says Nadine. 'After all, it *is* the ANZAC picnic.' For Nadine, who spends most of her leisure time riding pillion on her boyfriend Rueben's Harley Davidson and rarely spends time with the family these days, is a stickler for certain rituals. 'And now there's Helge ...'

Helge, who isn't exactly sure what an ANZAC picnic is, smiles again. She has found merging into her host family, albeit it a small one, an adventure, and she and Nadine get on well.

The girls take Lance's old Wolseley down to the supermarket, leaving him to the dishes. He flicks the radio back to Concert FM and humming along to a Strauss waltz, buffs each glass and plate to a sheen. When the phone rings, he's quick to take the call. 'Rueben. ... Is everything OK? ... How bad? ... And what about the bike? ... Bad luck, mate. Shall I get Nadine to come up? ... OK, tomorrow, then. ... Sure, I'll tell her. Take care.'

He puts out his hand to open the study door, then changes his mind. Instead, he fetches a newly turned kauri bowl, tucks it between his knees, and begins working in a fine film of linseed oil.

'It's hopeless,' says Cynthia, emerging from the study and raking her fingers through her hair. 'I've checked the figures again and again, but I just can't get them to come out right.' Lance sighs, knowing what this is leading to, and knowing it will be just him and Helge going on the ANZAC picnic. The very thing he fears.

The drive from Geraldine to Peel Forest passes through gently rolling farmland. They could be driving through an English country estate, muses Lance. The trees are English, the houses are English, as are most of the animals. Autumn light delineates each tree, and the colours flare lemon, orange, tangerine and lime. Marmalade trees raining peel.

Helge's watching the trees, too. Autumn came as a shock to her. She'd seen pictures of New Zealand bush on travel posters, but those trees were always green. She reaches for her shades, her hand lightly brushing the wheel.

As he drives, Lance is becoming increasingly aware of the closeness of Helge's leg, the closeness of her bronze skin. The chill of the Swedish climate must make her immune to cold, he thinks. Whereas Nadine covers up with the same greasy jeans, the same sloppy tops, all year round, Helge dresses in airy layers. And she's one for jewellery. Lance glances at her three necklaces — one bone, one copper and one shell. He notes how Helge's garments flow over her body like shavings of wood.

Little by little Helge feels more at ease. She's so happy driving through this beautiful farmland, neither of them speaking, each comfortable with their own thoughts. And she's thinking in English today. This is a recent change. She'd been through a confusing time of thinking partly in Swedish, partly in English – a mish-mash of ill-matched words and broken ideas. It helps that there are just the two of them. She's secretly glad. She misses Nadine, of course, and is sorry about Rueben's accident. And poor Cynthia left at home with her spreadsheet and her frown. Cynthia makes her nervous though – makes her words stick in her throat. But Lance ... well, he's just a huggy old bear.

Helge's own father was rarely at home and, on those odd occasions they were in the apartment together, he was either plugged into his laptop or cell-phone, whereas Lance always has time for people. Helge smiles at him. But he's looking hard at the road.

They slow as they approach a small town. 'We're coming into Peel Forest,' Lance says. Helge is surprised to see a group of kilted pipers tuning their bagpipes outside the village hall and looks questioningly at him. 'It's the ANZAC service,' he says.

They leave the tarseal and climb a row of khaki hills, then descend into the Rangitata Gorge. Blue mountains wrap them in clean air and the flat plain between is braided with silver strands. Helge catches her breath. The farmland is green for a time, then bleaches to dun brown. As they pass Mt Peel, White Rock, Rata Peaks, Forest Creek and Ben McLeod stations, she jumps her finger along the map. Ben McLeod, a tall, gaunt pile of rock, frowns down the curve of his beak, like a hawk guarding his road-kill. As his shadow reaches out to the car, Helge shudders.

'It's lonely up here, all right,' says Lance, 'but beautiful.' He feels more at ease now he's broken the silence. 'They get a lot of snow – can be completely snowed in some winters. Must've been a difficult life before the road went in. Where would you like to picnic?' Helge, who is absorbed in the new landscape, doesn't answer. 'There's an anglers' track along a bit, or we could drive right up to Mesopotamia.'

'I'd like that,' she says, with that little smile again.

Lance suddenly hates that smile. When he first met Helge that day at the airport, when she walked into the terminal, flashing her smile and swinging her slim hips, he'd thought her worldly, sophisticated. But knowing her better now and discovering that first impression was just a veneer, he feels ashamed of the stirrings she'd aroused – the stirrings that are still there.

Helge is thinking about picnics. Although Stockholm is blessed with parks, her family's not a family for picnics. She'd had such fun preparing for today, had felt like a Christmas child as she and Nadine selected and packed the food into the cane hamper. She'd carefully folded the worn gingham cloth, filled the flask with hot water and packed the chilled drinks. Helge smiles at Lance again. Such a bear of a man with his bushy beard, crinkle eyes and low-slung paunch. She has a sudden urge to hug him. She isn't normally a demonstrative person – rarely touches her own parents, hasn't since she was a child – but right now she feels like giving her host dad a big squeeze.

Beyond Ben McLeod, the river flats fan out again and at the head of the valley, the snow-flecked Alps peer through a giant V. But to Helge, the snow seems as if it's painted on, for the air is warm and easy to breathe.

They judder across the cattle-stop and pull up just past the Mesopotamia Station boundary fence. Lance flings open the door, strides across to the fence and marvels at the braided river. He opens the boot and takes out the hamper, rugs and cushions, setting them out with a sense of urgency. The perfect place, the perfect setting. Birds sing a high tune. Lance lies back on the rug with his head on a cushion and draws steadying breaths, then watches Helge as if through a camera lens.

She spreads the cloth and begins to set out the ANZAC picnic. She, too, feels different – each stretch of her arm, each twist of her neck is in slow motion. Her fingers curl round the cheese like the tendrils of a vine. 'Shall I pour you a ginger beer?' she asks. The brown bottle is beaded with condensation.

'A kiss first,' Lance finds himself saying, and as he pulls Helge towards him, his camera freeze-frames.

Helge is quite happy to kiss him and snuggles into his cushioned chest. But her kiss is a mere flutter and glances off his parted lips. She gives Lance a quick squeeze, then slips from his arms. 'Uncle Bear,' she chuckles, then snaps the ginger beer tab.

Helge notices Lance is very quiet on the drive home. He's such a

173

restful man, she thinks, and sits back in the worn leather seat, still savouring the picnic tastes, the wide views, the clean air.

Outside, the light shuffles back to the hills, highlighting each fold. Helge thinks they look like an old army greatcoat, but when the gorge presses in, she sees rents in the woollen fabric and grey bones poking through. The poplars are bare here, and their shadows barcode the road. And at Peel Forest, when the podocarps join to become one large shadow, she shivers and reaches for the rug to cover her skin.

Cynthia comes out to meet them. She's changed into a long sarong and has washed her hair. 'Did you have a nice picnic?' Her voice has lost its pinched tone and moves easily through the night air. As she kisses Lance above the tide-line of his beard, Helge sees him cringe. 'Nadine called from the hospital,' says Cynthia, opening the boot. 'They're keeping Rueben another night, but apart from a cracked rib, he's fine.'

'And his bike?' Lance asks.

'Not critical,' Cynthia says with a shrug. 'Helge?' She raises her brows at the tartan rugged girl. 'Is everything all right?'

Helge lets the rug fall. 'There were shadows,' she begins to explain, then loses her words. She stands still for a time, her eyes fixed on the back of Lance's head. Then she lifts the hamper from the boot, and moving lightly, carries it through to the kitchen, where she unpacks the remains of the ANZAC picnic.

An earlier version of this story was broadcast by Radio NZ.

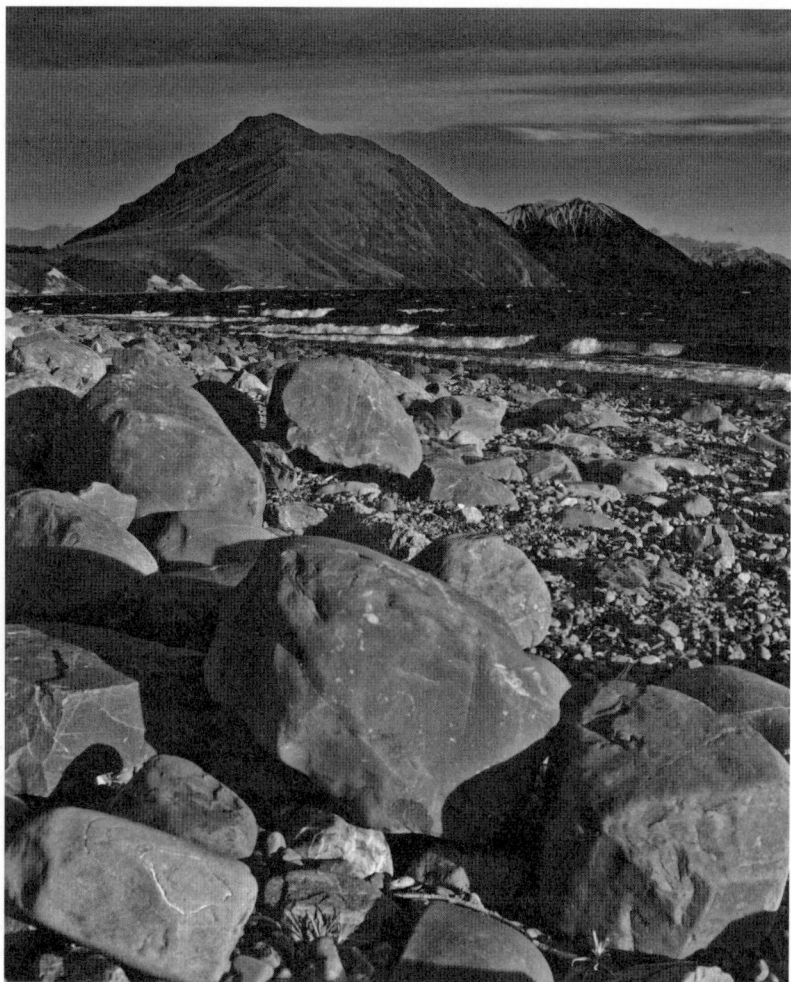

High Country

'Listen to the silence,' ...

– Geoffrey Hooker, 'Breakfast at Lake Lyndon'

Inland

Jane Myhill

lush green, ripe
in the summer heat
bush climbs the hill

fierce wind
scents the gorge
with lupin

a hand span
of alpine flowers
takes hold

grey stones
with white
striations

rivers
within
a river

First published in *Kokako* 5, September 2006

Requiem in a Town House

Owen Marshall

Fiction

Mr Thorpe came off sixteen hundred hectares of hill country when he finally retired, and his wife found a town house for them in Papanui. Town house is a euphemism for a free-standing retirement flat, and retirement flat is a euphemism for things best left so disguised.

Mr Thorpe made no complaint to his wife when he first saw the place of his captivity. She had accepted a firmament of natural things for forty years, and he had promised her the choice of their retirement. Yet as the removal men brought those possessions that would fit into the new home, Mr Thorpe stood helplessly by, like an old, gaunt camel in a small enclosure. Merely by moving his head from side to side he could encompass the whole of his domain and, being long-sighted by nature and habit, he found it hard to hold the immediate prospect of their section in focus.

It wasn't that Mr Thorpe had come to the city determined to die. He didn't give up without a struggle. He was a farmer and a war veteran. He went to church on Sundays with his wife, and listened to the vicar explaining the envelope donation system. He joined the bowling club, and learned which side had the bias. But he could not escape a sense of loss and futility even amid the clink of the bowls, and he grew weary of being bullied by the swollen-chested women at afternoon tea time.

Mrs Thorpe developed the habit of sending her husband out to wait for the post. It stopped him from blocking doorways and filling up the small room of their townhouse. He would stand at the letter-box, resting his eyes by looking into the distance, and when the postman came he would start to speak. But the postman always said hello and goodbye before Mr Thorpe could get anything out. There might be a letter from their daughter in Levin, a coloured sheet of specials from the supermarket, or something from the *Reader's Digest* which he had been especially selected to receive. It wasn't the same as having a decent talk with the postman though.

The town house imposed indignities on Mr Thorpe: its mean conception was the antithesis of what he had known. To eat his meals he must sit at what appeared to be a Formica ironing board with chrome supports. It was called a dining bar. After a meal Mr Thorpe would stand up and walk three paces to the window to see the traffic pass, and three paces back again. He would look at the knives in their wall holders, and wonder at his shrunken world. He had to bathe in a plastic water-hole beneath the shower. His arthritis prevented him from washing his feet while standing, and he had to crouch in the water-hole on his buttocks, with his knees two more bald heads alongside his own. He thought of the full-length metal and enamel bath on the farm. Sometimes he even went further back, to the broad pools of the Waipounae River in which he swam as a young man. The bunched cutty grass to avoid, the willows reaching over, the shingle beneath. The turn and cast of the water in the small rapids was like the movement of a woman's shoulder, and the smell of mint was there, crushed along the side channels as he walked.

In the townhouse even the lavatory lacked anything more than visual privacy. It was next to the living room: in such a house everything, in fact, is next to the living room. Mrs Thorpe's bridge friends could hear the paper parting on its perforations, and reluctantly number the deposits. Mrs Thorpe would talk more loudly to provide distraction, and her husband would sit within the resounding hardboard, and twist his face in humiliation at the wall.

The hand-basin was plastic, shaped like half a walnut shell, and too shallow to hold the water he needed. The windows had narrow aluminium frames which warped in his hand when he tried to open them. The front step was called a patio by the agent, and the wall beside it was sprayed with coloured pebbles and glue.

The section provided little comfort for Mr Thorpe. The fences separating his ground from his neighbours' were so vestigial that he found it difficult not to intrude. One evening as he stood in the sun, like a camel whose wounded expression is above it all, he was abused by Mr McAlister next door for being a nosy old fool. Mr Thorpe was enjoying the sun on his face and thinking of his farm, when he became aware that he was facing the McAlisters as they sunbathed on a rug. Mrs McAlister had a big stomach and legs trailing away from it like two pieces of string. 'Mutton-headed old fool,' McAlister said, after swearing at Mr Thorpe over the fence. Mr Thorpe turned away in shame, for he was sensitive concerning privacy. 'Oiy. Go away, you nosy old fool,' shouted McAlister.

After that Mr Thorpe exaggerated his stoop when he was in his section, to reduce the amount of his body that would appear above the fences, and he would keep his eyes down modestly as he mowed the apron lawn, or tipped his rubbish into the bag.

He tried walking in the street, but it was too busy. The diesel trucks doused him with black fumes, and most of the children used the footpaths to ride bikes on. The pedestrian lights beckoned him with Cross Now, then changed to Don't Cross whenever he began.

Mr Thorpe took to sleeping in the garage. In the corner was a heavy couch that had been brought in from the farm, but wouldn't fit in the house. It was opposite the bench on which he'd heaped his tools and pots of dried-up paint. At first he maintained a pretence of occupation between bouts of sleep, by sorting screws, nails, tap washers and hose fittings into margarine pottles. As his despair deepened he would go directly to the couch and stretch out with his head on the old, embroidered cushion. It was one place in which he didn't have to stoop. He had an army blanket with a stripe, for he had begun to feel the chill that is of years, not weather. There he would lie in the back of the garage; free from the traffic, the McAlisters, and the confines of his own town house. He had always been able to sleep well, and in retirement he slept even better. He was granted the release of sleep.

Mr Thorpe would lie asleep with his mouth open, and his breath would whine and flutter because of the relaxed membranes of his mouth and throat. His face had weathered into a set configuration, but it was younger somehow when he slept. His wife played bridge in the living room with her friends, or watched programmes of glossy intrigue. Mr Thorpe lay in the garage and revisited all the places from which he had drawn his strength. Age is a conjuror, and it played the trick of turning upside down his memory, so that all he had first known was exact and fresh again, and all the things most recent were husks and faded obscurity. Mr Thorpe talked with his father again, soldiered again, courted again; yet when he was awake he forgot the name of the vicar with whom he shook hands every Sunday, and was perplexed when asked for the number of his own town house. Waking up was the worst of all. Waking from the spaciousness and immediacy of past experience, to the walls of his small bedroom closing in, or the paint pots massing on the bench.

'He sleeps all the time, just about,' Mrs Thorpe told the doctor, and Mr Thorpe gave a smile that was part apology for being able to sleep so well. 'He must sleep for sixteen or seventeen hours of the twenty-four sometimes. He sleeps most of the day in the garage.'

'Ah, he's got a hideaway then,' said the doctor. He used a jocular tone, perhaps because he was afraid of the response to any serious enquiry. Let sleeping dogs lie is a sound enough philosophy. 'You need more sleep when you're older,' said the doctor. He'd forgotten that last time Mrs Thorpe came on her own account, he'd told her that old people don't need as much sleep.

'And he hasn't got the same energy anymore. Not the energy he once had. His interest in things has gone. Hasn't it, Rob?' Mr Thorpe smiled again, and was about to say that he missed the farm life, when his wife and the doctor began to discuss the medication he should have.

He never did take any of the medicine, but after the visit to the doctor he tried briefly to interest himself in being awake, for his wife's sake. He sat in front of the television, but no matter how loud he had it, the words never seemed clear. There was a good deal of reverberation, and laughter from the set seemed to drown out the lines before he caught their meaning. He could never share the contestants' excitement over the origin of the term *deus ex machina*.

A dream began to recur. A dream about the town house in Papanui. In the dream he could feel himself growing larger and larger, until he burst from the garage and could easily stand right over the house, and those of his neighbours. And he would take the town house, all the pressed board, plastic and veneers, and crush it as easily as you crush the light moulded tray when all the peaches have been eaten. Then in his dream he would start walking away from the city towards the farmland. He always liked that best in his dream. He was so tall that with each stride he could feel the slipstream of air about his head, and the hills came up larger with every step, like a succession of held frames.

He told his wife about the dream. She thought it amusing. She told him that he never could get the farm out of his head, could he. She said he should ask McAlister if he would like to go fishing.

In the dream Mr Thorpe never reached the hills: he never actually reached where he was walking to so forcefully. But he seemed to be coming closer time by time. As he drew nearer, he thought it was the country that he knew. The hills looked like the upper Waipounae, and he thought that he would soon be able to hear the cry of the stilts, or the sound of the stones in the river during the thaw, or the flat self-sufficient whistle made by the southerly across the bluffs at the top of the valley.

Owen Marshall: *The Master of Big Jingles* (John McIndoe, 1982); republished in *The Best of Owen Marshall's Short Stories* (Vintage, 1997)

An Eye for the Birds

Mary Bell Thornton

You go on I said
I'll wait here

I lay on the side of the Craigieburn track
trying to decide if the little birds
feeding in the canopy were wax eyes
They never did come close enough

Upon his return
he put down his pack and picked
up a small red flower
Look at this. A rare mistletoe
Only grows between here and
Broken River

I'd looked up for an hour
and never saw it
He took the opportunity and kissed me

Sun

Rachel McAlpine

a slice of sun
on a mountain top
this is the source
of the light

a man with feet
of melted rock
he flies me
like a kite

Rachel McAlpine: *Lament for Ariadne* (Caveman, 1975)

Ashley Gorge

Mark Pirie

It was the year that Def Leppard
was big. 1987. The album appropriately

titled Hysteria and I was playing it
as loud as possible in my ears.

I was in the back of a car. It was a family
trip; around New Year's, we were heading

to Ashley Gorge for a picnic and a swim
in the river. My sister was there in a bikini

starting to flower. I was nearly 14. Together
we played with our younger cousins while our

grandparents sat in the shade. Our parents
kept watch over us, taking us to the river

to swim. We laughed, smiled. Nothing bad
happened, no accidents or scares. It was

just a nice day. My sister even borrowed
the Def Leppard tape from me and

started listening to it, too. Why I mention it
is for the happy time it represented.

Around us: bees, birds, water, pebbles, ripples,
yells, yelps, gorse, bush – and the scorching heat.

The forest giving us its colour and warmth – just as
it must've done for others, too.

185

Breakfast at Lake Lyndon

Geoffrey Hooker

Fiction

So tell me again why I agreed to all this,' Marie said as the rain began
to lash down upon the windscreen.

'Come on, it'll be fun,' Greg replied, straining his eyes to see through
the murk that was enveloping them as they drove out of Christchurch.
'The weather will be much better once we get over the Pass.'

'I thought we'd do something special on our anniversary. This doesn't
seem very romantic to me.'

'Our anniversary's not until Tuesday. We can do something then
if you like.' Greg decelerated as the car hinted it was on the verge of
aquaplaning.

'But it's thirty years ago today.'

'*Sergeant Pepper told the band to play.*' Greg smiled at his wife.

'I just thought we might do something special tonight … like a candle-lit dinner.'

'We can have a candle-lit dinner up at the lake.'

'If this rain keeps up, tonight's dinner will be cold baked beans in our car.'

'Lighten up.' Greg tweaked the windscreen wiper knob to maximum speed. 'Just think, thirty years ago today we had that magical night at Lake Lyndon.'

'My mother couldn't believe I was off to spend my wedding night in a tent,' Marie laughed. 'I don't know … you Cantabrian men, you're one of a kind.'

The rain had all but stopped by the time they entered the village of Springfield and blue sky greeted them as their car began to ascend Porters Pass. The snowy peaks of the Torlesse Range glistened in the late afternoon sunshine.

'See, I told you the weather would be okay up here,' said Greg. 'The Canterbury south-westerly takes on a different persona once you get inland.'

Within twenty minutes, they pulled up beside the lake. The late autumn sun had already set behind a mountain that flanked the western shore.

'Do you know what I like most about this place?' Marie helped her husband lift the dinghy from its trailer.

'Well, it can't be the hoards of hotels and shopping malls,' Greg replied.

'But that's just it,' Marie replied. 'This place is the same as when we camped out here on the 13th of May, 1978. Nothing's changed.'

'There's a few less fish in the lake.' Greg attached the oars to the dinghy. 'Or maybe they're just getting harder to catch.'

'What's the spade for?' Marie asked, as her husband loaded the boat. 'You've never bothered digging a long drop before.'

'You'll find out,' he smiled.

'You're not planning on burying me are you?'

'All will be revealed.' Greg screwed up his face to appear demonic.

They set off across the lake to their favourite spot.

'Am I on track for the Sacred Rock?' Greg asked, after he'd been rowing for a few minutes.

'Aye, aye, captain,' Marie replied. 'Sacred Rock dead ahead, Sir.'

Within another few minutes, they arrived at the bay opposite their car. Marie unloaded the boat while Greg pitched the tent on the grassy verge below a rocky outcrop.

'Listen to the silence,' Marie sighed, as she sat on a deck chair beside her husband in the late twilight.

'We've had some grand times here, haven't we?' Greg said. 'Skating with the kids. The marathon swim. Do you miss those days?'

'You mean the good old days?'

'Do you miss being a family of five?' Greg turned to face her.

'We're still a family of five,' Marie replied. 'We're just scattered around the world now … but, yes, I do miss them.'

'The kids used to love it here,' Greg stared out over the calm lake. 'I think the best time I ever had here was that weekend in '91.'

'When I was too sick to come. Thanks a lot!'

'I didn't mean it like that,' Greg laughed.

'Louise told me a couple of years back that something really special happened that weekend … and that one day I would understand what it was. What did happen?'

'Ah ha,' Greg said. 'Bedtime.'

Shortly after midnight, Marie was woken by the distant sound of voices and car doors slamming. She unzipped the tent door.

'What is it?' Greg mumbled.

'We've got neighbours. I hope our car's okay.'

'Go back to sleep. It'll just be fishermen.'

Marie managed eventually to stop worrying about their car and drifted to sleep again. She woke to a crisp clear morning and peered out at the snow-capped Big Ben Range. Greg was already dressed. Beside him, Marie looked across at an array of tents. 'I can't see any fishermen.'

'Are you ready for your surprise?' Greg handed her the spade. 'Remember Mike's addiction to Raiders of the Lost Ark?'

'Yes … but what do I need a spade for?'

'That weekend in '91 when you didn't come, Mike insisted we bury treasure.'

'What? Where?'

'At the foot of the Sacred Rock.' Greg pointed at the bank behind their tent.

'And I get to dig for it?' Marie looked puzzled. 'Today?'

'Off you go.' Greg could hardly contain his excitement.

'Shall we have breakfast first?'

'No time for breakfast,' Greg replied. 'Try digging about a foot out from the bank, directly below the Sacred Rock.'

Marie did as she was told, and ten minutes later she called, 'Treasure!'

Greg smiled. 'Tell me what you've found.'

'This old Coca Cola bottle.' Marie's voice was quivering with excitement. 'With a note in it.'

'Go on, read it.'

'*Dear Mum. Today it will be the second Sunday in May, 2008. Dad says it will nearly be your 30th wedding anniversary, so this is our gift for you. It's 1991 where we are, but today we made a special promise to each other. No matter where us kids are living at the time, on the second Sunday in May, 2008, we're going to surprise you. We're all going to come to Lake Lyndon! See you then, love from Louise (aged 11), Amelia (aged 9) and Michael (aged 7).*' Tears were streaming down Marie's face. 'Is it true?' she asked.

'I damn well hope so.' Greg hugged his wife tight. 'Happy anniversary,' he whispered.

'Are you lot coming over, or what?' they heard from the other side of the lake. 'Breakfast's ready!'

Remember
for Ian 1933–2006

Lesley Ayers

Remember childhood?

The long days of summer
skies arching wide
over mountains

Remember

the heat of the wind
in December
gusting and blowing
tugging at tussock
trying our tempers
teasing the iron on the roof

Remember

the wide
braided river we swam in
splashed in its coldness
scattered its crystals
with breath-catching laughter

Remember the echoing
notes of the bellbirds
filling the air in
the warmth of the sun

Then
the quietness of night
when the wind dropped
the taste of trout
from the fire's embers

while smoke
drifted up

And we lay on our backs
under black velvet skies
counting millions
of shimmering stars

Your river, your mountain, your land.

Two rivers, two worlds:

the strong flowing Thames
the oak and the thrush
the cold northern wind.

But always –
the mountains
the wide skies
the river
would call you back home
to soft weeping rimu
the wind in your face
and the songs of the stars

Remember

Castle Hill

Tom Weston

The jawbones of dead sheep
snag on grasses, worn incisive

by the floss of the mountain's storms.
These are their teeth in the yellow gum

of the clenched hill, picked over,
muscle buried under tussock and matagouri,

slight echoes of the
limestone corrugations on the skyline.

Damaged shrubs struggle
into cracks above the reach of sheep

where the earth folds
into a shock of eating, and not just teeth here

but the stubble of broken jaws, armies of jaws,
limestone molars splayed across the yellow hill,

indentured to storms,
fast in the plate of the earth.

Tom Weston: *The Ambiguous Companion* (Hazard Press 1996)

Keas

kimbala

Three black silhouettes
against the morning sun.
Zero one – zero two – zero three.

Wheeling in, to
eyeball us from a swollen lip
of crusty snow
the edge of the day-lodge roof.
Go ahead –
dip a head, ex-pose a downy bum,
charm us with your hop-a-long dance.
Measure mouthful by mouthful,
the eater; the eating.

'Hobble on hook-beak.
No-one is going to feed you.'

Never Forgotten

Barry L. Smith

Don't know where you ended up
old reprobate off the mutton chain
out of season whitebaiter
anywhere south of Okarito
dirty old bugger, someone said.

I see you now, bag coated
back bent, digging spuds
while stolen hogget boiled inside
your rust-roofed hut

planning the weekend hunt.

Returning early from the back hut
on Sunday afternoon, you said
you'd take Charlie's boy out
the high route over open tops
where you knew deer would be.

Searching bush margins
in late afternoon you passed
across your rifle, scoped
the delicate neck reaching
into broadleaf; she fell.

'You finish the work, boy' you said
showing the slow steeling of blade
wrist rolling to gain the right angle
using the outward stroke to form
the smooth sound;

Pointing where to cut, where to punch
the skin away, using the knee,
finding the right spot to break joints;
boning out, folding the skin.

Never forgotten, loading the packs
striding together, men's strides
down the last ridge.

On a High in the High Country

Judith Doyle

When Dan Shand was a sixth former at boarding school, he did a project on his family's sheep and cattle station in the High Country of the Hurunui district, inland from Kaikoura. He pictured tramping over Island Hills Station, exploring the sub-alpine heights, crossing the streams that S-bend through the property and staying in bush huts in the back of beyond.

After some years living overseas, he came home and set about putting his dream into practice. It took two and a half years to research, plan and build ... the 30km Hurunui High Country Track. Judith Doyle, in a group of older trampers from Wellington, walked the track towards the end of 2007.

Mandy Shand, with little Amalia, who was six months old at the time, takes the six of us to the start of the track, near their 1882 homestead and the ex-shearers' quarters where we'd spent our first night ...

It's November and this is the High Country, so I'm well wrapped up against the nip in the air, which soon takes the form of hesitant hailstones and then light floaty snowflakes. Repeat – snowflakes! And I'm not a hale and hearty tramper, more the Johnny-come-lately variety.

Soon we're climbing up into Finland – well, a large plantation of Douglas firs, to be exact. But the drifting snowflakes make the scene look very Scandinavian and other-worldly, transforming the dark gloomy conifers into cheerful Christmas trees.

At one point a large hairy wild pig crosses our track, with a youngster scuttling behind. We continue climbing, sometimes in snowflakes, sometimes in hailstones, until we reach the highest point of the track. From here, we see fold after fold of mountains, including the Organ Range, so-called because erosion has carved the hillsides into 'organ flutes'.

It's tough country to farm. At the morning briefing, Dan had told us that Island Hills Station, despite being 7100 hectares, is not really financially viable. 'If it's flat and green, it's probably not our land,' he laughed. Today's walk is a graphic demonstration of that.

The rest of the day we walk up and down, up and down. We cross many streams, their music competing with the song of the numerous bellbirds. We have two avid bird-watchers in the group and their enthusiasm is infectious.

A sign on a tree directs us to a shelter with scrumptious muffins and thermos flasks of tea – a personal touch that is typical of this enterprising young couple. With care for the environment in mind, they have also placed a toilet here and at a few other strategic points.

Soon we run into mud. There may be less than 200 cattle on this station, but they must all have decided to tread and defecate on this stretch of track. The mud/manure sucks at our boots. My feet are reminding me with each step that this 14.6km walk – much of it over rough ground – is a bit much to ask of them. The following week, Dan worked on this stretch, he told me later, re-locating the worst stretches and putting shingle on other parts.

Finally we're at Valley Camp. There is a large expanse of grass with a brook babbling through it; a cosy little cabin on one side of the stream (built for mustering in 1933) and a larger, newer hut – our accommodation – on the other.

Boots off, tiredness forgotten, we sit on the deck in the sun enjoying the snow-streaked mountain on one side and bush all around us. My contentment is sealed by a gorgeous hot shower, a log fire, a wine in hand and the knowledge that it's not my turn to cook dinner …

The sun warms us next day as we climb up and up to the snow fence, built in the 1930s to prevent sheep moving to the tops in the winter and being caught in large snowfalls. Packhorses were used for carrying fencing gear then and for mustering.

We see some bush orchids, the little green native clematis and, higher up, alpine-daisies – not in flower right now. Later, we walk through beech – red, mountain and black, the latter with encrusted sooty trunks. I steer clear of these, in case wasps, attracted to the sweet sap, might still be feeling hungry …

As we approach Bush Hut, I tread for a while on a shagpile of thick springy moss. There are ferns and foliage everywhere under the trees. A haven of green. And this is where our bush camp is located. There are a log cabin, built in 1932, a hotwater shower camouflaged in the bush and three double tents on wooden bases. A large table is situated under a roof hung with mesh curtains that can be pulled around against the sandflies, and there is a well-equipped little kitchen.

When the sun sets, the cold returns with a vengeance. We dine on a right-royal risotto in the log cabin, beside a fire in a giant fireplace. In albums are fascinating bits of family and local history – Dan's great-grandfather bought Island Hills in 1928 – but the story that amused us that night was the convoluted tale of how a Samoan tapa cloth came to materialise on the wall.

Blue Lagoon, so-called, greets us next day, early on in the walk. The bush enclosing it has crept closer over the years and turned it khaki. Never mind. It's a pleasant, peaceful place to linger.

Beside the Mandamus River we meet Dan on transport duty. Packs and chillibins are strapped on the trailer of his farm bike. In front of Dan perches Biddy, the family's perky Jack Russell/fox terrier cross.

This last day is the easiest and shortest. We saunter along the farm tracks and across pastures, looking over to the hills alight with golden broom. I see paradise ducks squawking above us and the occasional hawk, but our birdwatchers pick out the more elusive birds: brown creepers, spur-winged plovers, redpolls and pied oystercatchers. A gentle finish to a track that's challenging in parts, immensely varied in landscape, well constructed, and which gives a glimpse of the life and challenges of High Country farming.

From an article published in the travel pages of the *Dominion Post* (19.12.2006); *Waikato Times* (21.1.09) and *Walking New Zealand* (Issue 112, 2007)

Korimako
Anthornis melanura

Karen Zelas

on a morning clear
as a bell

'melodious wild music'
Cook ventured
'tunable silver sound'

dull green-brown
honeyeating diva
competes

with possums for tree-
              blossoms
berries
          fruit
                    insects
in season

surround sound

Note: Korimako, *Anthornis melanura*, is the bell-bird (from NZ Bird series).

High Summer in Canterbury

Lorna Staveley Anker

Summer on the upland
               does not come with
               halcyon arch,
nor hay-hung noon
warming tousled tussock –
but with those tiny,
tawny butterflies,
like yachts they dip
larupping tipsily
on gazania-golden
shards of wings,
prised from soft-smouldering
stained windows
of an ancient cathedral.

Lorna Staveley Anker: *My Street Lamp Dances* (Lorna Staveley Anker, 1986)

Crackbone Carries the Lamb

Claire Hero

CRACKBONE carries the lamb
The lamb
bleats himself into silence

effluvia in the throat-hold, earthwarm—

Sheep cleaved
from the mountainside

Spore of sheep, wind-bred,
spread, springing up

in clutch & tussock, fun-
gal, many-footed, blight of teeth

Sheep at the sea edge, reef
of driftbone, saltwhite

the amniotic scree
out of which I walked
on the grey rock on the red rock

—Shepherd my tongue into the pen
Crackbone carries lamb.

Claire Hero: *Sing, Mongrel* (Noemi Press, 2009)

No Flowers

Barry Southam

Fiction

Garth Grenhall grew up in a rural environment in Canterbury, part of a farming family whose ties to the area went back several gener-ations. He was the only son of four children, so there were expectations.

One of these was rugby. Which presented a problem. Succeeding in the national sport was never an option for Garth due to his light weight and awkwardness. He suffered badly from a lack of co-ordination, the result of his parents' misguided idea that dominant left-handed chil-dren should be forcibly changed to right-handed because the world was designed that way. His attempts to control the odd-shaped ball drew scathing responses from his father, as paternal disappointment overflowed from the sideline.

Garth's co-ordination problems also contributed to his mechanical ineptitude with any farm implement. The pain of correction from a heavy ruler on the knuckles for clumsiness at the dinner table was matched by paternal scorn at his vain attempts to assemble things, or even work out which way nuts screwed or unscrewed.

'My son, captain of the awkward squad,' his father would announce to anyone in listening distance.

The school yard was no sanctuary for Garth. His unfortunate initials meant he was nicknamed 'horsie' and was neighed at by both the boys and the girls, in between being dead-armed, foot-tripped, held under in the school baths and having his lunch stolen.

Garth's father tried various methods to mould him in his own image, before deciding that he was 'not a chip off the old block, not even a piece of bloody sawdust,' when describing him to a visiting relative, loud enough for Garth to hear. 'About as much use on a farm as a fart at a funeral,' was another favourite.

At age twelve his father bought him a powerful air rifle for Christmas, much to Garth's surprise. Presents until then had been largely practical or useful. The gun was a distinct departure, but Garth could only guess at the significance. After giving it some thought, he settled for it being part of the making-a-bloke-out-of-him campaign that his father had not yet totally abandoned. Garth tentatively tried the gun out on some tin cans on one of the stock yard fences, with some success, deciding that he quite liked the sense of power it gave him, as well as the feeling of achievement as the cans flew in the air with a resounding 'ping' each time he hit one.

On Boxing Day, the family went camping at the Waimakariri river mouth, a relative agreeing to look after the farm for a few days while they experienced life under canvas and had a break for the first time in years. The next day two thrushes sat enjoying the sun on a pine tree branch close to their tent. Garth's father thrust the airgun into Garth's hands whispering, 'Sitting ducks, lad. Get em.' Garth knew better than to argue, so aimed deliberately too low.

To his chagrin, a slight upward jerk of the air rifle on firing saw one of the thrushes drop to the ground, very dead. He ignored his father's rare praise, and was 'off his food again' at the evening meal. For days afterwards the other thrush sat on the same branch, calling mournfully for its mate. Garth found it hard to bear and sold the rifle to a neighbour's son a few weeks later. The lack of selling permission and the punishment that followed meant he could not go to school for the first week of term while the bruises subsided.

Garth had one friend, Patrick, but it was a friendship that had to weave its way through a thicket of parental abuse, Patrick being 'a bloody Mickey Doolan' and someone who was certain to get him into trouble. At times he was forbidden to have anything to do with Patrick for offences that ranged from stealing fruit from a neighbour's tree, to being caught in the hay barn smoking. The latter had been good for a six-month ban, after the usual beating.

When the ban was lifted Patrick was very careful when Mr Grenhall was around and watched whatever he said or did. He had increased his watchfulness after a late night smoking session when Garth told him about Raggles, the family pet.

Garth had raised Raggles from a straggly, soaked and abandoned lamb, after a big storm that had seen quite a few stock losses. He was always delighted by the way Raggles would run to him, whether he had a milk bottle or not, wagging his tail furiously. And how he would be waiting for him by the big gate when he came home from school. He loved Raggles, his only companion at that time.

One evening as they finished eating, his father announced how delicious the meal had been and that the meat they had just consumed was Raggles. Garth sat disbelieving and looked to his mother, shaking his head.

'You are joking, aren't you, Charlie?' his mother asked.

'Nope,' his father replied. 'Not joking.'

'Oh, Charlie, how could you?'

'The lad needs to know the realities of farm life. Far too soft in the head.'

Garth ran from the room, hysterical.

Years later, Garth's new bride was puzzled that he was not attending his father's funeral. She asked his best friend Patrick if he knew why, after Garth refused to discuss it. Patrick shrugged and changed the subject. She became more concerned when Garth refused to send flowers or a card. She realised she did not really know the man she had married.

First published in *Southern Ocean Review*, October 2006

Did the Company Agent Have a Heart

Lorna Staveley Anker

You would never guess,
reading his spidery entries
from October 1880, and through
the next eighteen months,
that the uplands and plains
of early Canterbury ever
yielded beauty, colour, form.

This perennial traveller visited
grand and lesser stations
which still endure. Longbeach
his favourite, Race Course Hill,
Craigieburn, Mt Bruce runs,
White Rock – many others flowed
from his strong J nibs.

And, like infant water-races
these lists thread leisurely through
shearing, pasture conditions,
flax swamps, stony paddocks,
farm building, ploughing,
cocksfoot and hay crops
and accounts done by lamplight.

Not even a verbal sigh for
the thistles and gorse and
bad ditches at Doyleston;
then a dutiful mention of the
accident in Mr Grigg's trap,
and all without headline.

Engrossed by the details in
the cost of each wire staple,
how someone transferred
four hundred and ninety-eight
three-quarter bred weaners,
and the diarist slept well
after endless accounts were returned
to the company in the young city of Christchurch.

Then – the first lapse on
February 21st 1881, he notes
'Sent a wish to J.A.'
That sultry Monday may have dragged
as he shod the horse, Punch.

A year later, with seasonal accuracy,
the writing pulses black and clear
across the page, in February.
He has met Laura again
after six years
'and this evening
dined there again,
and went to the theatre
with them, and bid her another
long goodbye after the play.'

Did the company agent
have a heart?

Gorge Hill

Louise Tomlinson

The shearers
sit
for morning cuppa
under the
milky froth
of the elderberry.
Black tea.
Pink iced buns
and chunky
fruitcake.
Cigarette smoke.
Blue haze
and high above
a hungry hawk.

Heartland

Pamela Wade

A memoir

The wire fence ran straight across the metalled road. Mum turned off the Morrie's engine and we got out into the sudden silence. All around us were the bare brown hills of the North Canterbury high country. To one side a stream picked its way along a gully set about with isolated cabbage trees. Dense woolly mats of panting sheep lay in their sparse shade. There was no sign of a gate.

We looked at each other. It had been a long hot trip from Christchurch, and neither of us had ever shone in adversity. Accusations and recriminations were on our lips, when we heard the approaching roar of a vehicle and around the bend ahead appeared a dusty Land Rover filled with dogs. It came straight at us, slowing only slightly as it hit the chain link fence which, with much squeaking, lay flat on the road as the truck passed over it, and sprang up again behind, undamaged.

The driver hung cheerfully out of his window. 'Island Hills, you want? Not far now. Just rip into it!' and he roared away again, leaving us choking in his dust. We cautiously eased the car across the fence, understanding now the complicated arrangement of wires, posts and springs on either side of the road, and found that our destination was in fact just around the corner.

The homestead was a long low building, part stone, part wood, wrapped around with a wide veranda and set apart by a barrier of lawn from a motley collection of barns, sheds, kennels, workers' quarters and shearing shed. Behind them all was the reason we were there: the sorting yards where a dozen or so horses stood patiently dozing, swishing their tails against the flies and waiting for their next expedition through the hills and river valleys that gave Island Hills its name.

I thought 'Heaven' would have been more appropriate. For the next three days, I sat happily on a dapple-grey horse, suitably named Lucky, as he took me along winding trails, through damp green bush and clear rivers, up and down impossibly steep and rocky banks, over wide flat meadows and to the tops of hills I would have called mountains if the Southern Alps had not towered above them in all their snow-capped glory.

This trek had everything I could have wanted: horses, independence (Mum had trundled away again in the Morris Minor), friendly companions, long days in the sun, and glorious scenery; and ever since, I have loved the open, rolling brown hills that stretch from Marlborough to Otago. Later, in all the years that I lived overseas, whenever I was asked if I missed home, it was not beaches that I pictured, nor the lumpy green lushness that surrounds me now in Auckland, but the wide, empty spaces of the high country, the shimmering edge of the tawny gold summer grass where it meets the clear blue of the sky, the spiky, unsociable cabbage trees and the dramatic limestone outcrops that cluster on hilltops like crenellated castles.

It was a time of heightened sensations: there could be nothing finer for a horse-mad twelve-year-old than waking in the early morning to the call of the bellbird, wriggling into shorts and T-shirt on my bunk, and sneaking out of the log cabin into the fresh, cool green light of a

205

new day, padding quietly through the beech forest with a handful of halters to fetch our horses.

Sometimes it was a long walk to find them in the diamond-bright light of a clearing, but the reward was a gloriously solitary and triumphant ride back, knees wet from brushing through the bush, bottom damp from sitting on a dewy horse. Fantails and robins flitted along with me, catching insects disturbed by the horses' hooves; besides their twittering, there was no noise louder than Lucky's occasional snort. For a while, this fresh and unspoilt world was mine, and it was perfect.

Then the smell of wood smoke and bacon would overwhelm that of horse and humus. It was the signal that the others were up, and the rest of the day was filled with simple food, laughter, sunshine, sweat and scenery. The night was for resting tired muscles, poking at the campfire and telling stories, while the dark thickened behind our backs and the stars pricked out patterns above us.

This idyll lasted for only three days, and I have never – yet – returned to the high country on horse-back; but I went again as often as I could on my own feet. I found that tramping increased the pleasure of the same delights: I valued the long views even more when they were hard-won by my own effort. And as I grew older, I discovered one more benefit in the wide and sun-bleached landscape:

There is a purity in those open empty hills that refreshes the soul, something about the scale of the surroundings that lightens the heart, eases the mind and shrinks problems to a manageable size. It is an ancient comfort, and the words that express it best are also very old: I will lift up mine eyes unto the hills, whence cometh my help.

First published in *North & South*, February 2003

High Country Days

Barry L. Smith

On these high country days
the sky with its stark
raving sun presses down
on the canopy of bush
where footsteps
on moss
are crisp

blowfly days
with a trickle of sweat,
last week's leg
of venison
hangs motionless
from the crook
of an elbowed bough

on these high country days.

Previously published in *Micropress New Zealand*, Vol. 3 Issue 3, 1998 and Barry L. Smith: *Always A Little Further: poems of mountains and valleys* (Barry Smith, 2004)

One Green Bottle

Nancy Cawley

Fiction

Rain: roaring on the iron roof of the hut, spitting down the chimney to hiss into the ashes and creep in widening pools from the four wet-darkened packs on the floor. Soon the rain would bring an early dusk and the hills would press closer. She shivered and pulled a jersey from her pack. It was time for another brew.

The three men sat around on the bunks, reading ancient hut magazines with tired relish; learning Why Teenage Bridegroom Coshed Landlady, or How to Make a Coffee Table From a Barrel – a respite from the sodden mountain world and the scruffy hut.

They had arrived in the early afternoon, nudged down the river by veils of nor'west rain and threatened by the mumble of boulders in rising streams. Two weeks of climbing behind them and the mountain camaraderie wearing thin – high days on sunlit snows forgotten in the long trudge home. Oh lord, to wallow in a bath again and lie between sheets. She'd had enough of George's ponderous musings on the weather, Hugh's off-key singing, Mike's belches. She wanted to be home.

'Who's got the milk powder?' Claire asked.

Keeping his eye on his *Women's Weekly*, Hugh groped in his pack, produced a battered tin and handed it to her.

'Thanks.' For nothing, she thought.

The crumby remains of lunch still littered the table, some cheese, half a packet of shattered crackers, aluminium containers with various deteriorating contents and a fly swimming in a tin of sardine oil. She cleared a space for the mugs. Three mugs. 'Where's yours, George?'

'Um? Oh,' he fumbled at his feet and produced a plastic mug with Donald Duck on it.

Hugh threw his magazine on the bunk and stretched, clenching his fists and stiffening his arms in front of him. 'Oaah!' he yawned, his bristly jaw moving sideways with the effort. 'What about coming out for a shoot before tea, Mike? This bush doesn't go up far.' He jerked his head in the direction of the green wall rising behind the hut. 'Then there are good open terraces.'

The water in the blackened billy began to boil, bubbling and hissing at the edges. Claire lifted it off with a drying sock and threw in the tea. The sudden fragrance made her think of clean cups and scones. She filled the battered mugs and handed them round; she had mixed the milk powder carelessly and small lumps floated on the top. The tea tasted good, but billy tea never tasted as good as it smelt.

'Bring back some liver if you can, Hugh,' she said. 'Be good for breakfast.' The hot drink had cheered her, but really, a dirty hut in storm-drenched mountains was an absurd place to spend the last night of a holiday.

'I'll see what we can do. You've got that bit of venison for tonight, right?' He didn't wait for a reply; the two men took their parkas from the nails behind the door and Hugh slid his rifle over his shoulder. 'See you later.'

Their murmuring voices dwindled and died. Claire went to the door and looked out. The rain had stopped, but soggy clouds lay like a collapsing tent on the tussock flats. The wet grass glistened and somewhere a steady drip pinged on a tin. Behind her George said, 'That low ceiling of cloud could be a good thing. I remember once in Jagged Stream ...' He rambled on, one of many stories illustrating his infallibility as a prophet of conditions meteorological.

'Perhaps I'll get some firewood before dark,' Claire said. Solitude, she must have solitude.

'No, she'll be right. I'll get it. I want to look at those lacebarks anyway.' George sloped away across the grass and, in sudden exasperation, she poked out her tongue at his retreating back.

Claire turned into the silent room, shadows already lying in the corners and the fire a riffle of grey ash. She shuffled the magazines together, dumped them in a carton and slid it under a bunk. With the table cleared, she spread a bit of cheese on a biscuit and ate as she worked, sweeping the twigs and chips from the hearth and floor, the puddles drying into long smears on the floorboards. As she threw the sweepings onto the fire, it gave a startled hiss and threw up an orange flag of truce. A few more sticks and the fire was burning again, lighting an almost cosy room.

It had been dark for a while by the time the men returned. By then Claire had a venison stew simmering, and in the hot ashes at the side, a scone loaf in the hut's caste iron camp oven. The men had shot a hind and brought back the liver. George had collected two sizeable loads of firewood and now sat in the doorway, ringing out shingle-ridden socks and humming softly. Hugh started to clean his rifle outside and Mike squeezed past George into the fire-lit room. 'Something smells good.'

'Scone loaf,' said Claire.

'Yeah? Clever kid.' He draped his socks over the wire above the fireplace, then began rummaging in the shelves by the door. 'Anyone seen any kero around? Thought we might get this old lamp going.' Nobody had. George was searching now, too, but it was Mike who found it, the flat green bottle with the whisky label.

'Wonder if this is it?' Mike lifted it to his nose. 'That's not kero! Smells like … Heh, Hugh, what's this smell like to you?'

Hugh came in slowly, propped his rifle in the corner, took the bottle and sniffed. He and Mike looked at each other. 'Oh, brother,' said Hugh softly, and they both smiled. For once the label was right. They all knew it would never happen again, not with a whisky bottle anyway; a third of a bottle.

After the meal, cupping their mugs and sipping carefully, with George playing now and again on his mouth organ, they began to talk of next year's trip, next year's mountains.

An earlier version was published in *The Listener*, 20 July 1962

Stag

Claire Hero

What doesn't fear my hands? The crush of my thumb, my fingers that make a fence. The deer stand on one side, watching. Among the trees they are hard to see, their skins smell of leafmould. If they would let me, I would trace the grain of their pelts, its marks like a secret language. I would put my hands upon them, and their eyes would roll white.

—And then we are in a green room, the stag and I, his brown eye turns like a globe, leaves fall around us.

The leaves, then the trees.

The trees fall around us. We watch them through the window. The trees fall, and then the deer fall. I want to speak, to stop this, but my voice box, I see, is in the palm of my hand, closed as a seed. First the antlers fall, then the hides dry up and blow away and the bones erode until they are only eddies of sand. The stag closes his eye.

Out of the wreckage, deer-shapes of light rise and walk toward us. They walk through the window, they walk through the wall, they walk through every fence I make between us.

．．．．．．．

. . . the antlers are heavy.
They drip blood into my eyes.
They bow my neck until I am doubled,
until I am savage, and forest, and endless.

Claire Hero: *Sing, Mongrel* (Noemi Press 2009)

An Inimitable Stag

Judy Boyd

A memoir

That looks like *sixteen* points!'
So it's *his* yodelling that lately disturbs our sleep. I've never seen a more magnificent stag, but sadly, with this peerless antler display, he may have signed his own death warrant.

'You should go and see him, Peter. His antlers are about a metre high.'

Peter glances up from his crossword and says, 'I've told you a million times; don't exaggerate.'

The stag gets used to my daily visits, ambles up to the fence, nearly close enough to touch. He holds me with a magnetic gaze; his eyes are beautiful, amber, with fake-looking eyelashes. I could stand there for hours.

There have always been deer next door; what's so compelling about this particular animal? I can't explain; I feel chosen, enchanted, and delude myself that he feels it, too. But then he's shifted to a back paddock and I miss him. My husband doesn't. This ridiculous emotion, wasted on a stag, is something he can't control ...

My husband ... that's it! It's the same magnetic spark that passed between us when we first met fifty-four years ago. When I blushingly mentioned that 'love at first sight' phenomenon to a psychology lecturer, he'd laughed and said, 'No, it's pheromones; their smell. It's what subconsciously attracts or repels when you meet someone new.'

But a stag's pheromones ... would they engender a similar effect?

Peter is grateful when the stag is shifted and he can do his *Press* crossword uninterrupted by daily stag stories. He throws me a clue to console me.

'What's a seven-lettered word for 'meantime'?

'Interim.'

Soon the stag's back in his front paddock. With the mist closing in, and perfectly centred under a low-hanging rainbow, it's like he's just stepped out of a nineteenth-century painting. Donald is cutting poplar poles on which the stag will polish off his last velvet fragments. He drops the axe when I appear, and wipes his sweaty brow on his sleeve. Fantails flutter around our heads chasing the insects he's stirred up.

'Donald, that stag is stunning.'

'Yes, but he's here just for the breeding season. He's promised to some Americans.'

'Will they take him to the States?'

'No. After the mating they'll shoot him. Mount his head ...'

A cloud passes over the sun and the birds quieten; even the golden pheasant patrolling the fence line stops squawking. As though listening, the stag closely observes us while idly flicking at flies with his inadequate tail. 'You can get about $5000 for a head like that.'

Dismayed, I visualise the stag browsing, the hunter walking up to the fence, raising his rifle, fixing his sights ... the stag slowly turns, sensitive ears pricking at the click of the bolt. I imagine that regal head as a macabre trophy, the focus of fatuous lies about deer stalking.

I'm shocked, walk away, grateful for the lyrical notes of a passing bellbird embroidering this tranquil scene.

When gardening one morning I hear gunshots, but Donald reassures me.

'No. The stag's been shifted to another paddock where he's busy expanding his gene pool.'

There's the stag, just down the road. Like a voyeur, I peer through the poplars; I can't resist watching as he roars lustily, rounds up his thirty concubines, and herds a reluctant mate into the far corner. The stag heaves his enormous weight up onto her and, after a few hearty thrusts at his target, a great shuddering racks his body. Remote as a prostitute repairing her makeup, the hind goes on eating grass, while the stag, grunting with pleasure, collapses at her hooves. All that candelabra stacked up on his head must make it hard work, plus the daunting prospect of fertilising another twenty-nine hinds …

The stag shreds the expensive shade netting around his paddock. His antlers have hardened to bone with ivory points; his coat gleams in the sun, but his hinds all cower under trees at the far end of the paddock. I'm embarrassed at my prurience, hope no-one's watching me, and ask myself, 'How can they resist him?'

Hanging heavy as incense, that unmistakable gamy stink of a stag in rut pervades the air.

'Peter, the stag's by himself in the corner, right by the road. I should've taken the camera today.'

My husband hugs me and I'm aware of his faintly musky aroma.

'Well, he's probably waiting for you to come back. Get on your bike and go and photograph him.'

So I bike along with the camera; the stag is still there, but his hinds mill around. The light is wrong; he looks away, and it's hard to get a perfect shot.

When Peter spreads these photos over the dining table, he's shattered. 'If I'd known you were going to take seven shots of that bloody stag, I'd never have suggested it,' he grumbles.

When the stag next sees me, he trots over. Fantails flick around his antlers, but he ignores them. I feel smug; he *does* know me, but today there is a flinty spark in his eyes. He glares, and shakes his gorgeous head at me. In frustration he grunts and bucks, then charges at the high square-netting fence between us. He can't attack, but those wicked points stabbing through the wire indicate he doesn't want an audience. Then he catches a different scent; his head thrusts forward, his mouth widens with a monstrous roar, and he bounds off to herd his harem again.

When I get home, Peter says, 'I've just heard a radio programme about deer farming. They said stags at mating time see humans as a threat to their dominance over the herd.'

I say nothing.

Another season passes and the stag is still there. Donald is retired now, a full-time deer farmer. I meet him at his letterbox one day.

'The poplars have started shedding their leaves.'

'Rust,' says Donald, flipping through his mail.

'I see the stag has shed his antlers.'

'Yes. Wait here – I'll get them for you.'

He's soon back with the antlers piled up on his farm bike tray. I note they've lost tips off some spikes.

'I wasn't exaggerating; they are over a metre tall.'

'Pick one up,' says Donald, grinning.

'Lord! I can't even move it.'

The stag's broad shoulders further widen under my newly respectful gaze. 'Imagine the strength of his neck, supporting these.'

Donald nods. 'He's already started growing new ones.'

The fawns, bleating their loneliness, cluster around when I come along. They've lost their spots and look cute, sporting their first, tall velvet spikes. Graceful on long, slender legs, their guileless eyes and tender ears remind me of Walt Disney's film *Bambi*, which I saw as a child.

The stag stands proudly aloof in his new set of antlers, thick with velvet.

'Ye Gods! That's *nineteen* points.' No wonder I am overawed by this rarity of the cervine world.

Donald rubs the top of his head as though feeling for his own antlers. 'He'll be roaring soon and going out to the hinds. Then we'll de-antler the weaners and they'll go to Belfast Freezing Works.'

Swamped with misery I visualise the newly velveted fawns, forever denied the delights of procreation, fearfully slipping and stumbling up the ramp into the double-decker truck, slithering down again on arrival, workers prodding as they hold back, splay-legged in the works race, the butchers waiting with their stun guns ...

Stop it! They're not your animals, I remind myself.

When next I see the stag his antlers have long, blackened shreds of dried velvet dangling like streamers on a Christmas tree. His stance is urgent, sniffing in all directions. Sounding like a carillon of church bells, his lonely bugle echoes in the night, serenading his hinds in a distant paddock.

As if in rehearsal of the coming cervine nuptials, leaves shower like confetti across the paddock in a gusty southerly. I gaze at the stag through the thinning poplars as he tears at the tattered shade-cloth fence, scraping the last strings of velvet from his antlers.

'Peter, the stag's torn off a metre square of shade cloth. It's draped across his antlers like a wedding veil, and he's blinking and twitching like a bartered bride. Perhaps he'll break a few points again in trying to pull it off ...'

We meet Donald in town one morning. 'Where's the stag?' I ask. 'I haven't seen him for ages.'

'He must have been trying to get in with the hinds,' Donald says, 'and he broke that electric wire on top of the deer fence; it flicked off and wound round his antlers and he got tangled high in the willows trying to scrape it off. Thank God I found him or he'd be dead now.' He looks stricken at the thought.

Peter, who dislikes emotional displays, waves at Donald, grabs my arm, and hurries me away. Later, when I'm walking, I meet Donald mowing his grass frontage.

'How is he?' I ask.

'Pretty weak.' He walks over to the fence, peers down to the willows where two plovers screech at their wayward chicks, and comes back, saying, 'When the vet came, she administered two shots of tranquilliser before we could cut him down.' He looks thoughtful. 'He could hardly stand, and he's due to start mating ... I kept going round with the tractor all last night to make him stand up, or he might've died.'

I note the irony, but cross my fingers and ask, 'Did he break off any points?'

Donald grins at me, swings back onto his mower, saying, 'Fortunately, no. He isn't finished here yet.'

The next balmy autumn morning I'm hanging out the washing. There's no threat of winter, apart from the fantails. I shake some bushes to stir up insects for them. They flit and twitter around me and I wish they'd stop using Peter's shirts for target practice. A helicopter passes over, and disappears behind the poplars, the clack-clack of its rotor blades slowing to a stop. I hear men's loud banter echoing across the paddocks.

A breeze rustles by, and more leaves drift down. I envisage a vastly overweight American, more accustomed to city skyscrapers than rural landscapes, lumbering out of the helicopter, exchanging his cigar for a rifle, waddling over to the fence …

All is suddenly quiet. I wait, hardly breathing and bury my face in one of Peter's damp singlets, seeking his gamy essence. Like a bad omen, two blackbirds haggle over a stretched out worm.

When the shot finally comes, it sounds unnaturally close.

The air squeezes out of me. I am choked by dread. I rush inside. 'Peter! *Peter*! They've *shot* him!' I scream and scream again, 'Where are you? *Where are you, dear?*'

Winter in the Mackenzie Basin

Sandy Nelson

Fog sneaks across the grass
Searching fingers stretched out.
It swallows our town,
Turning tussocks into white rainbows
And pines into silent ghosts.

Days later the mountains send their breeze
To claim the flat land back.
We look at them and say hello.

A week later
The white monster is back.
It came silently at midnight,
Tiptoeing down the street
And into our back porch,
Wetting our shoes
And stealing our smiles.

Saturday morning,
The long drive to rugby.
Frost and fog and black ice,
Lake Pukaki lost behind
A thick white curtain.

Leafless poplars reach for a hidden sky.
We cautiously crest Simons Pass.
The road is a slick inky ribbon,
Our truck a green snail on wheels.

An orange glow spears our eyes.
The sun says good morning
To a huddle of hungry cattle,
To a distant farmer on a red tractor,
To snow covered peaks,
To us.

Family Ski Hut at Craigieburn

Mary Bell Thornton

Separated for a week
You up the mountain
Me down here

I close my eyes and hear
the snow ridding kick of the toe
of your boots on the step

The rattle of the kerosene heater
as you fire it up in the morning

The view through beech trees
from the dunny with no door
across the valley to a mountain of virgin snow
Time it right and the sun rises as you sit
If world leaders
crapped up here there would be no wars

I see you walking the short track to the spring
to fetch nature's best (unbottled) water
Hear the mocking cry of kea
looking for an open window

The hiss of the Coleman lamp persists
as icicles melt in your whisky
the aroma of your gourmet mountain meal
momentarily overrides
the smell of kerosene
Even here, it makes my eyes well

No, I'm not weeping – I just remember that's all

The click clack of your ski boot clips
chattering of the day ahead

You ride the rope tow
up the slope – the one they call
The Big One or simply The Burn
You hold the nutcracker, ride higher and higher
the silence broken
by the grinding tractor engines
in the tow sheds
At last you reach the top
the only sound your breathing

I remember when we were young
Gluvein, hot toddies
And once the children were asleep
uninhibited passion
in the boot room by the fire

The small basin we bathed in

You up the mountain
And me and my knees down here

An earlier version was published as 'Craigieburn' in *boulder writers 2* (Boulder Press, 2008)

Thoughts from the Boulevard
Ohau Ski Area

Sandy Nelson

My thighs are screaming.
I stop.
I look.
What is this word in my head?
An obsolete airline.
A small freshwater duck.
A greenish-blue colour.
Lake Ohau.
Teal.

Midwinter Christmas 1888

Neville Guthrie

Fiction

Two squares of orange light shone from the kitchen windows of the Burkes Pass hotel behind him. In front all was total darkness, not a single star to be seen, just the crunch and feel of shingle to tell him he was on the road up to the pass.

It had been a good party. Trust old George to organise a good party for McMiddlemas. Bobby wasn't sure about that word, whether George had just made it up. George was like that, came out with all manner of statements confidently proclaiming them as truth, but sometimes you wondered. He wore odd socks, too. McMiddlemas, George had insisted, was an ancient word meaning 'Mid-Winter Christmas' especially for people in the southern hemisphere. As most Mackenzie Country shepherds, station hands and boundary keepers, like Bobby, had emigrated from Britain or had parents who had, they knew about Christmases in mid-winter.

'Why don't we have a Mid-Winter Christmas here in Burkes Pass?' George had asked. Not expecting or waiting for an answer, he just went ahead and arranged one; the first Saturday in July would be a good day for it. Barney, the publican, entered into the spirit of things by getting large bunches of holly tied up either side of the fireplace and rolling up little balls of red paper, which he stuck among the leaves.

George spread the word, and station staff from far and near began arriving from late morning. Bobby met blokes he hadn't seen for months, in some cases more than a year. He consumed a few beers sitting in the sunshine then, after a hearty hotel dinner, he had a whisky. It really warmed him up, so he had another. The weather had turned cold. Barney lit the fire and they pulled up a semi-circle of chairs around the big black log-filled fireplace. They were enjoying yarning so much that when Barney warned it looked like they might be in for some snow, nobody moved. They just kept on reminiscing about old times, old friends and families, horses and dogs.

All of a sudden, Bobby, who had just downed another whisky,

blurted out, 'I don't remember my name.'

'Course you do. It's Bobby.'

'I mean my proper name.'

'Well, what was your father's name?'

'It was Robert, too.'

'Yeah, but Robert who?'

'That's what I don't know. I've never used a family name. I've always been just Bobby.'

'Where are your parents now?'

'Both dead years ago.'

'Brothers and sisters?'

'Never had any. Always been on me own. The only kid at our school that never had brothers or sisters to get Christmas presents for. Sometimes we didn't even have Christmas at our place. My dad reckoned it was hardly worth it just for one.'

'But you can't go through the rest of your life without a proper name,' exclaimed Jock.

'Right!' agreed George. 'We should give you one.'

'What? Here, now?'

'Yes,' they all chimed.

'Right, Bobby No-name.'

A dark high-backed carved armchair was placed in front of the blazing fire. Bobby was seated on it, and a sprig of holly ceremoniously stuck in his tartan tam-o-shanter, like it was a Christmas pudding. Barney offered a half empty bottle of beer and George proceeded to sprinkle Bobby with its contents while loudly proclaiming, 'In the presence of your friends here assembled, with their wholehearted blessing and support, in the true spirit of McMiddlemas I bestow upon you an appellation which you shall proudly bear as the title of you and your kin from this day forth unto eternity. I hereby name you Bobby Robert Whistlebritches.'

'What's with this Whistlebritches, George? I want a proper name.'

'A proper name, Bobby? A proper name! Whistlebritches is not only a name that's proper, it's a name that's ancient and honourable; it's Celtic and has a touch of magic about it. You see the Whistlebritches of old were said to be in touch with the little people.'

'What little people?' Bobby asked, shaking beer from his headwear.

'Oh, all manner of elves, goblins, fairies, McWilly witches and so on.'

'What on earth are McWilly witches?'

'Oh, they're beautiful fairy witches, who ride small heather brooms and only do good things for people.'

'And how do us Whistlebritches get in touch with these little people, then?'

'You don't. They get in touch with you.'

It was very dark, very late when Bobby slowly headed out into the cold night air. It sure felt like snow and his feet were not working so well; they tended to stumble off to the left every now and again. This was a worry for he well knew there were deep water-worn ditches alongside the roadway, down which rushing rainwater found its way to the Tengawai River. More than one poor soul had perished in one of these on a dark night.

The squares of light behind grew smaller; an icy breeze came swishing through tussocks from the south. Bobby pulled his coat collar up and plodded doggedly onward into the lonely darkness. A tiny glimmer of light showed way up ahead; what could that be? Too low for a star. Walking became so much easier with that little glowing something to aim for. The glow increased as he neared it and he realised the strangest thing: it came from a small person in pointed red hat, red pants and matching pointed shoes. This little fellow wore a glowing golden coat and had smiley wrinkles all over his face. With a cheery greeting the stranger shook Bobby's hand and went on past. A slightly dazed boundary keeper carried on into the uphill blackness and it wasn't long before he stumbled to the left again.

Thud; a sudden sharp blow to his left thigh. He swung around bewildered and came face to face with the little red-hatted man, standing there, smiling.

'You kicked me, you mingy little brat,' Bobby roared, and stomped off up the road. When he'd recovered from the fright, he realised another glimmer of light had appeared ahead. On reaching it another little man stood before him, this time wearing a green hat above his glowing golden coat. When a third glimmer appeared, Bobby turned to look behind and there were Red Hat and Green Hat, both following him closely. Effects of the lateness of the hour, the large dinner and possibly the whiskey as well, caused him to waver drowsily toward a ditch again.

Thud; a swift kick brought him up short and got him heading straight towards a third little man in a red hat. The next one had a green hat and that's the way they alternated all along the road. By the time Bobby crossed the pass, he had a small army of glowing coats behind him, and they could all kick! Frozen flakes of snow driven by a wailing wind were stinging his face, building up on his coat and finding their way down his neck by the time he reached the shelter of his hut.

Before closing the door he looked back. Acting as one, the little men reached up to remove a sprig of holly from their hatbands and plant it at their feet.

Next day Bobby woke late. Outside the sun was shining on a knee-deep blanket of glistening snow. Going out in his Sunday jacket, he cleared snow from his old log seat, spread a dry sack on it and sat down to enjoy the sunshine. Just then a figure appeared. It was Danny the drover. He'd been kept on by the boss to do odd jobs round the station during winter.

'Gidday, Bobby, how would you like a holiday?'

'A what?'

'A week off. The boss sent me up to give you a spell for a week. He says you can go down and spend the time fixing up those sheep yards by the dip. Be a bit of a change for ya.'

'Would it ever! A whole week with real people to talk to.'

Danny had brought bread, cheese and cold roast beef. They sat and ate a meal together as a brilliant alpine sunset set the sky ablaze with pink, red and flaming orange banners of cloud, streaming east from dazzling white peaks.

What a great weekend. Now he was getting a break at the homestead.

'If this is a Whistlebritches' McMiddlemas,' Bobby thought, 'it's wonderful. I wish I'd been a Whistlebritches years ago.'

Or was he dreaming? But then, how could he explain the long straight row of holly bushes growing by his hut?

Another Day

Barry L. Smith

Today you climb to find
no perfect arête

nor summit cairn, damn it,
only horizontal wind and rope, no hope.

Another day, you may return
to ride the ridge, that bridge

between the fears of mountaineers
and the casting out of doubt.

Previously published in *New Zealand Alpine Journal* and Barry L. Smith: *Always A Little Further: poems of mountains and valleys* (Barry Smith, 2004)

224

Aorangi/Mount Cook

Rachel McAlpine

the westerly scrapes
the core of the land
the blade of the mountain
spare

milk and water sky
rolls into my hand
we should walk naked
in air so pure

Rachel McAlpine: *Lament for Ariadne* (Caveman, 1975)

About the Authors

Amelia Anderson (12 years) attends Rangi Ruru Intermediate School. She enjoys playing the flute, hockey, cricket and creative writing. She had two Haiku published in *Before the Sirocco* (NZ Poetry Society, 2008).

Lorna Staveley Anker (1914–2000) was a Canterbury poet, writing from her 50s into her 80s, and called 'the first NZ woman peace poet' for her later works. She raised five children and three collections of verse, with work published locally and internationally.

Ruth Arnison's poems have recently appeared in *Deep South, Orbis, Poetry NZ, Poetry Porch*, and *foam:e*. In her free time she edits *Poems in the Waiting Room NZ*, an arts in health project, based in Dunedin. See http://www.pitwrnz.blogspot.com/

Coral Atkinson was born in Ireland and lives in Governors Bay on Banks Peninsula. In 2005 her historical novel, *The Love Apple*, appeared and was followed in 2006 by *The Paua Tower*, both published by Random House NZ.

Lesley Ayers has had poetry, short stories, children's stories and travel articles published in New Zealand, Australia and Canada. She enjoys walking, travel, coffee and friendship. Palmerston North is home, but she spent high school and university years in Christchurch.

Brigid Barrer grew up in Christchurch, the daughter of second generation New Zealand parents, an Irish-English father and a Tainui-English mother. She worked in adult and child mental health and child protection for 30 years. Brigid lives in Auckland and has a 22-year-old daughter.

Jennifer Barrer was born in Canterbury, living on the Cashmere Hills. She has five collections of published poetry, and her work appears in anthologies. A mentor to many within the Arts, she is well known as an actress, director and teacher.

Maggie Belcher lives on the beach and comes from Weardale, County Durham. She loves music, art and walking the dog, Harry; writes fiction, nonfiction, poetry, short stories, and edits/tutors writers of first books.

Paul Bensemann of New Brighton, Christchurch, has worked as a community newspaper editor, in the parliamentary press gallery and as a radio reporter for Mana Maori Media. In 1981 he lived near his wife's uncle, Riki Te Mairaki Ellison-Taiaroa.

Tony Beyer has been writing and publishing poetry in New Zealand for several decades. Among his books are *The Singing Ground* (The Caxton Press, 1986) and *Human Scale* (Sudden Valley Press, 2002).

Judy Boyd grew up in Southland. She was a Karitane Nurse, then a Lincoln University secretary before completing a BA Eng, Hons at the University of Canterbury. She is married with three sons and is starting an MA in Creative Writing later in 2009.

Marisa Cappetta has lived in the USA, Australia and New Zealand. With guidance from mentor, Kerrin Sharpe, three poems have been accepted by *The Press*, Christchurch, in 2009. Because she is also a visual artist, she enjoys creating imagery in her writing.

Nancy Cawley is a Christchurch journalist and book-reviewer. Her travel memoir, *Divorced & Gone to Europe*, was published by New Holland Publishers in 2005. She is currently writing a second travel book.

Mary Keaveny Costello was born in London, emigrated first to Australia, and has now lived in Christchurch for 55 years. She is a former member of Mensa, the South Island Writers' Association and the Pegasus Writers' Group. She is married, with one son.

Ellie Cradwick (14 years) goes to St Andrew's College. Last year she won the ICAS writing assessment that she did through school. Her hobbies include photography and hockey, and some day she would love to bungee jump!

Lorelei Cropp is a former art teacher who lived for many years on a farm in the Blythe Valley in North Canterbury. She completed writing courses at the University of Canterbury to record her life for her two grandsons.

Judith Doyle writes on travel and the arts. She has written three travel books: *Pay for your Travel by Writing*; *Older and Bolder*, on outdoor adventuring and *Tea with my Tapas* on travelling in Spain. judith.doyle@paradise.net.nz

Doc Drumheller, born in Charleston, South Carolina, lives in Lyttelton, where he practises puppetry, music, poetry and edits and publishes *Catalyst*. He teaches creative writing at the School for Young Writers and has published five collections of poetry, most recently *Snake Songs*.

David Eggleton is a Dunedin poet and writer whose articles, reviews, profiles and essays have appeared in numerous publications. He has six collections of poems and another forthcoming; the first, *South Pacific Sunrise*, was co-winner of a PEN Best First Book of Poetry Award in 1987.

Bettina Evans is German, but, after 20 years in England, Ireland and Hawke's Bay, she is happily settled with her family in Lyttelton. She loves everything that changes and grows: plants and gardens, words and stories, family, friends and life.
Lesley Evans' first 16 years of life were spent in a series of small Canterbury towns and in the Christchurch suburb of St Albans where her story is set. She enjoys the process of writing memoirs for herself and for her family.

John Ewen has been writing for a number of years in several genres. Radio NZ has broadcast his radio plays, and he has been shortlisted and placed in several national short story competitions. He lives in Sumner, Christchurch.

Fiona Farrell has published three collections of poetry, short fiction, drama and six novels. She has received awards including the 1995 Mansfield Fellowship to Menton and the 2007 Prime Minister's Award for Fiction. She lives at Otanerito on Banks Peninsula.

Lois Farrow was born in Wellington, now lives in Christchurch. She enjoys people, the seasons, travel and her family, which includes two sons and seven grandchildren. Her writing encompasses travel writing, short fiction and telling people's stories.

Laurence Fearnley has published seven novels. *Room* was short listed for the Montana NZ Book Awards 2001; *Edwin and Matilda* was runner-up in 2008. She received the 2004 Artists to Antarctica fellowship and the 2007 Robert Burns fellowship.

Mary Fitzgerald's poetry has been published in *Takahe* and *The Press*. She has read at open mike sessions of *Catalyst* and the Canterbury Poets' Collective. She enjoys writing, as well as going into the mountains to tramp and breathe.

Adrienne M. Frater writes for both children and adults and her work has been published and broadcast in NZ and overseas. She lives in Nelson and writes in a study overlooking Tasman Bay and the Mt Arthur Range. For obvious reasons she sits with her back to the view.

Stephanie Grieve lives in Christchurch and writes poetry and short stories. She was a graduate of the Hagley Writers' Institute in 2008 and is currently completing the Year 2 Stage 2 course at the Institute.

Neville Guthrie is a retired builder, postmaster, retailer and technician. He has written several books and had short stories published in a number of anthologies. As president of South Canterbury Writers' Guild, he recently conducted a successful national short story competition.

Bernadette Hall is a widely published, award-winning Canterbury poet. In 2007 she was six months in Ireland on the Rathcoola Fellowship, giving rise to her latest book, *The Lustre Jug*. She is a founding staff member of the Hagley Writers' Institute.

Michael Hall grew up near Whakatane, but went to the University of Canterbury and currently teaches at Tauranga Boys' College. He plans to return south in the next few years, possibly, if he can afford it, after a teacher exchange to Canada.

Ruth Hanover comes to writing from a career in ESOL teaching in NZ, Cairo and Stockholm. She began taking writing seriously while caring for a mother with Alzheimers, returning to university for the creative writing papers. She lives in Christchurch.

Michael Harlow has published eight poetry books, including *Giotto's Elephant*, a finalist in the National Book Awards 1991, *Cassandra's Daughter* and *The Tram Conductor's Blue Cap* (Auckland University Press, 2009). Burns Fellow (2009); inaugural Caselberg Artist in Residence.

Siobhan Harvey is the editor of *Our Own Kind: 100 New Zealand Poems about Animals* (Godwit 2009). She is a writer, reviewer and the Poetry Editor of *Takahe*. Her partner is Aranui born and raised; Christchurch is her second home.

Jenny Haworth is a novelist and non-fiction writer. She has published three novels, *Hobsons' Chance*, *Lost Souls*, and *The Undone Years*, and several works of non-fiction, including *The Art of War: New Zealand Artists in the Field 1939–1945*.

Janice Healey lives in Christchurch. A member of South Island Writers' Assn., her poetry has been in *The Press*, *Takahe*, and a SIWA anthology. Her children's book, *Skateboards & Spaghetti* (Sunshine Books) appeared in 2009; a co-written collection is pending in USA (2010).

Claire Hero is the author of *Sing, Mongrel* (Noemi Press, 2009). Her poems have appeared in *Trout*, *Landfall*, *Tinfish*, and in many journals in the USA. After five years in Sumner, Christchurch, she now lives in upstate New York.

Geoffrey Hooker moved to Canterbury with his family in 1995. His first one act play, *One Short of a Black Short*, was performed in the Theatre Federation Festival in 2003. He has recently self-published two novels, *Hidden Messages* and *The Rag Doll*.

Jan Hutchison is completing a poetry collection, *The Coming of the Matariki*. Her poems are published in journals and anthologies, and her most recent book is *Days among Trees*. She and her husband, Hamish, enjoy time in the country.

Marissa Johnpillai is sometimes found pottering around gardens in Otautahi. She has studied and taught creative writing and has been published in New Zealand, Australia, Sri Lanka and the UK. Her several novels all look like poems.

Laura Keddell is a Christchurch writer, mother, journalist and former midwife. This is her first foray into published fiction, but she is beavering away in all weathers in her studio/caravan to complete her first novel. Last year she graduated from the Hagley Writer's Institute.

kimbala is the pen-name of a North Canterbury writer. A poet at heart, she is currently completing her first novel. She has been inspired, most recently, to write short stories under the tutelage of Helen Hogan at the WEA.

Belinda Lansley lives in Christchurch with her husband and two daughters. She loves to write, paint and cook and has a passion for vegetable gardening.

Stephanie Lester (8 years) won the 5–7-year-old class of a mudfish writing competition organised by Environment Canterbury in 2007. She won the 5–8 years section in the Northland Poetry Competition 2008. Writing is an important part of Stèphanie's life.

Helen Lowe won an inaugural Robbie Burns poetry prize in 2003 and has subsequently had poetry and short fiction published and anthologised in New Zealand, Australia and the United States. Her first novel, *Thornspell* (Knopf, 2008) is 2009 winner of the Sir Julius Vogel award.

Rachel McAlpine has been writing poetry for three decades, including ten collections of poems. Current poems are aired online (c-for-blog.blogspot.com). She lives and works in Wellington. Her main business is online training for web content writers, contented.com

Juliet McLachlan (8 years) is a student at Ilam School. She loves music, dancing, sport, art and writing. She has written many plays, stories, songs and poems.

Frankie McMillan is a Christchurch writer. She is currently working on a second collection of short stories but has been sidetracked by other literary forms such as poetry. Her first poetry collection is *Dressing for the Cannibals* (Sudden Valley Press, 2009).

Harvey McQueen was born in Little River in 1934. His career was in education but he is also a well-known poet (six volumes), writer (*This Piece of Earth*, 2004) and an anthologist, co-editing the best-selling *Penguin Book of New Zealand Verse* (1985).

Owen Marshall's awards include the Katherine Mansfield Memorial Fellowship, Robert Burns Fellowship, Montana Book Awards Deutz Medal, ONZM for services to literature, and an honorary Doctorate in Letters from University of Canterbury, where he is an adjunct professor.

Diana Menefy lives in Northland and writes both non-fiction (seven titles) and fiction (junior novels). Her articles and short stories for both children and adults have been published in a variety of magazines and anthologies and broadcast on the radio.

Robynanne Milford practices medicine with her husband and a great team at LAMC. In her other life she inhabits the world of poetry richly contributed to by guiding at the Christchurch Art Gallery, singing with the Cecilians and being the 'Dog' on their farm.

Jane Myhill lives in Christchurch. Her published work includes journalism, book reviews, poetry, photographs and opinion pieces. Canterbury's braided rivers are a continual source of inspiration to Jane, who likes rocks, driftwood and wide open spaces.

Sandy Nelson (previously Holland) lives in Twizel in the Mackenzie Country, which fills her with peace, awe and a feeling of timelessness. She is a teacher, mother of three boys and a beginning writer. Her main interest is writing historical fiction for pre-teens.

Sara Newman is a mother of four, a former volunteer with several community services, currently a guide with Christchurch Art Gallery. Her writing has been published in *Takahe*, *New Zealand Memories*, *The Press*, *NZ Pets*, and placed in a competition.

James Norcliffe has six collections of poetry, most recently *Villon in Millerton* (AUP, 2007). He co-edits *ReDraft* and is poetry editor for *The Press* and until recently for *Takahe*. His most recent fantasy novel for young readers is *The Loblolly Boy* (Longacre & Blackmore, 2009).

Karin O'Donnell hails from Johannesburg, South Africa. An ESOL and adult education tutor for over seven years and a professional non-fiction writer and editor since 2004, Karin has previously had short stories published, but this is her first published poetry.

Annie Orre was born and grew up in Christchurch, trained as a nurse, spent time in Australia, England and NZ and returned to Christchurch in 2002, now retired. She is married to her second husband and enjoys writing, painting, reading, movies and family.

Judith Paviell. Originally from Wellington, this long-time Mainlander is most at home in rural North Canterbury and lately Nelson, where she lives as a writer, poet, journalist, tutor, singer and cyclist. She has three adult children and one grandson.

Mark Pirie is an internationally published Wellington writer, with 21 books of poems, one of songs and one of short fiction. He is publisher for HeadworX. From 1995–2005 he initiated, co-edited and produced *JAAM* and currently edits *broadsheet*.

Jenny Powell is a Dunedin poet and secondary school literacy coordinator. She has three collections of poetry and has work in collaborative anthologies and in *New New Zealand Poets* (CD and book). Her next book, *Vietnam: A Poem Journey*, is due out this year.

Elizabeth Robertson has had poems published in *The Press*, *Takahe*, anthologies *Before the Sirocco* (NZPS, 2008) and *Splash* (the Airing Cupboard Women's Poetry Group, 2009) and been placed in competitions, including third in the NZPS Poetry Competition 2008.

St Andrew's College Year 3 Students: Apurv Bakshi, Sebastian Calder, George Foote, Helen Frogley, Victor Gan, Jessica Gavin, Sebastian Giesen, Molly Gower, Angus Loader, Juliette Newman, Philip Nordt, Kate Pennycuick, George Rutledge, Tyler Vandenberg, Logan Vincent, Jenna Wells, Elise Wilkinson, Anika Boet, Albert Chen, Harrison Dore, Libby Downs, Francesca Harrison, Tom Kepple, Andrew Kircher-Blay, Eva Kotzikas, Archie Macmillan, Ayla Marshall, Corban Matthewson, Galen Park, Grace Prodanov, Millie Thompson, Sam Tiller, Jenny Zhu.

Jane Seaford has been writing for many years. Several of her short stories have been placed, highly commended or short-listed in international competitions. Many have appeared in anthologies, magazines or broadcast on Radio NZ. She also writes novels.

Kerrin P. Sharpe has been published in *The Press*, *Takahe*, *Snorkel*, *Turbine*, *bravado*, *Poetry NZ*, *New Zealand Listener* and *Junctures*. One of her poems is in *Best NZ Poems 2008*. She won the 2008 New Zealand Post Creative Writing Teacher's Award.

Barry Smith has spent much of his time in the Canterbury mountains and has written poetry for 30 years. He is published in several magazines and his own collection, *Always A Little Further: poems of mountains and valleys*.

Barry Southam lives in his home town of Christchurch. He has had two books of poetry and two of short stories published, as well as many plays produced on stage, radio and television, locally and internationally. He is currently forming a film production company.

Janine Sowerby lives in Christchurch. She has had poetry and short stories placed in competitions and published in *Takahe, The Press, Kokako, Yellow Moon* (Australia), *White Lotus* (USA), *Albatros* (Romania) and NZ Haiku, NZPS and SIWA anthologies.

Barbara Strang was raised in Invercargill and now lives at McCormacks Bay, Christchurch. She holds an MA in Creative Writing (Vic). Her poems, haiku and haibun have been published here and overseas. *Duck Weather* was launched in 2006 and her next collection is due in 2009.

Tracey Sullivan spent her childhood in small-town Canterbury, studied at Canterbury University and lives for the moment in the Netherlands. She is a reader, writer, teacher and mother though not necessarily in that order.

Apirana Taylor is of Ngati Porou, Te Whanau a Apanui, Ngati Ruanui, Te Ati Awa and Ngati Pakeha descent. He is a short story writer, novelist and playwright, actor, musician, painter and storyteller. He frequently tours reading his poetry and has held residencies at Massey and Canterbury.

Campbell Taylor has worked in music, theatre and television and been published in several journals. Born and raised in Christchurch, he lives in Titahi Bay with his partner and baby girl.

Mary Bell Thornton has been published in *The Listener* and broadcast on National Radio, had a non-fiction book published, worked as a freelance feature and advertising writer for the *Nelson Mail* and *Leader* newspapers and is working on an historical novel.

Charlotte Trevella attends Rangi Ruru Girls' School. Her first poem appeared in *The New Zealand Listener* when she was aged ten years. She was a featured poet in *North & South* (March 2008); winner 2007, 2008 Junior NZPS competitions; a Foyle Young Poet of the Year 2008. Her first collection, *Because Paradise*, is due out in 2009.

231

Pamela Wade was born in Christchurch, and spent 17 years in England working as a groom, then teaching high-school English. Currently living in Auckland, she is a freelance writer, and in 2009 won the Cathay Pacific Travel Writer of the Year Award.

Janet Wainscott recently returned to Canterbury after a long absence and now lives and writes near Christchurch.

Tom Weston has published a number of volumes of poetry. A recent poem was collected in *Best NZ Poems 2008*.

Keith Westwater's poetry has appeared in *Landfall, Snorkel, JAAM* and other publications and has received or been short-listed for awards in New Zealand, Australia, and Ireland. He lived in Christchurch as a student during the years 1967–1970.

Julie Wuthnow, a former lecturer at Canterbury University, is a self-employed writer. She is originally from Seattle, and after living in California, Germany, Hawai'i and Finland, arrived in Christchurch in 1996. Her lounge features a clear view of Cashmere.

Helen Yong's poetry has been published in New Zealand, British, Australian and American journals and in anthologies, including the NZPS anthology and *the taste of nashi: New Zealand Haiku*. She enjoys the stimulating writing groups she belongs to in Christchurch.

Karen Zelas, born and raised in Wellington, has been 45 years in Christchurch. Coming later to writing, her poetry and short fiction have been in several anthologies, magazines and broadcast on radio. Her first novel, *Past Perfect*, is to be published late 2009. She is Fiction Editor of *Takahe*.

WILY PUBLICATIONS LTD.

Wily Publications is a small publisher dedicated to helping new writers find an outlet for their work. The main focus of the company is heritage non-fiction and we will occasionally consider historic fiction that is based in New Zealand or develops the experiences of New Zealand characters abroad.

Crest to Crest places the work of established writers alongside those who are still working to establish their reputation. It has been an exciting project and we received many excellent submissions – more than we could include in this volume. These have all been carefully considered and the final choice was made by the editor, Karen Zelas. The work she has chosen truly reflects the diversity in Canterbury writing.

I trust you will enjoy this selection and that you will support this publication so it will be possible to compile other, similar anthologies. The future direction of New Zealand publishing is in your hands. Support local authors and we will be able to build a great literary heritage and develop a much greater understanding of ourselves. We have the writers, but we still have to win the readers.

Jenny Haworth
Managing Director

FORTHCOMING PUBLICATIONS

Capturing Mountains: a biographical sketch of A.A. Deans, Nathalie Brown
A study of the life of Canterbury painter Austen Deans, with reproductions of a selection of the paintings he has completed over the course of his 94 years.

Past Perfect, Karen Zelas
A novel that intertwines the stories of two women: one a French settler of Akaroa in the 1840s, the other a present day Christchurch woman who comes to understand herself through exploring her ancestry, both in New Zealand and France.

Russian at Heart: Sonechka's Story, Olga and John Hawkes
A memoir about Olga's mother, who fled Russia after the revolution and lived in Shanghai, until finally winning the right to settle in the United States of America.

Swimming Upstream: the Story of Salmon Farming in New Zealand, Jenny Haworth
The story of how the industry grew from small, experimental beginnings to a multi-million-dollar enterprise, putting New Zealand salmon on restaurant plates and supermarket shelves here and overseas.

The Sacrificial Pawn, Peter Jackson
A memoir that relates Peter's experiences in World War II, when he was captured by the Japanese at the fall of Singapore. Now over 90 years old, Peter tells the incredible story of his survival.

The Undone Years, Jenny Haworth
Historic fiction set in the immediate aftermath of World War I. It opens with the Spanish Flu epidemic in Christchurch and then moves to Paris, Berlin, Vienna and Budapest.

If you are interested in receiving more information about any of these books
please email jjhaworth@xtra.co.nz